# The King's Wonderful Older Women

**Devotional Words
of Wisdom**

# Fiona Myles

**The King's Wonderful Older Women**

Bible passages are from the NIV, NLT, NKJV and KJV.

First edition printed and independently published in the United Kingdom 2023.

A CIP catalogue record of this book is available from the British Library.

ISBN (Paperback): 978-1-7392300-2-9
Imprint: Independently published
Typesetting: Matthew J Bird

For further information about this book, please contact the author at:
**Email:** fionamylesauthor@gmail.com
**Website:** www.fionamylesauthor.com

This book is dedicated to my incredible daughter
Georgie who one day will be able to read.

One day she will glean from the incredible wisdom and
encouragement contained in the pages of this book.

To Georgina
Thank you for your
grace & loving kindness
love Fiona
x

# FOREWORD

### *"The older I get the less I know"*

This is the quote I often hear around me in conversations, while people are longing and searching for truth and answers to a lot of life's questions. There is some profound value in quotes, we learn through our life's journey that we don't get all the answers to life's questions this side of eternity. As a nurse who has specialised in elderly care for thirty years, listening to people's life stories a lot and hearing all that they have learned. I have found that there is such wisdom in paying attention to the richness of the older person's wisdom, that they have gleaned over many years. To truly listen to people who have been through the different seasons of their lives with all of its beauty, pain, joy, and tears. With brokenness, loss, grief, and their personal redemption stories, that can be such a blessing and help you grow in your own journey.

As a fifty-two year-old Christian woman and Co-Pastor of Kings Church Salford I think it is absolutely brilliant that this devotional book is written by different women over fifty-five years of age, from their own personal journeys in life and their walk with their creator.

Take a few minutes from your day to pick up this book, sit and listen to those who are older or possibly in the same season of life as you are. I honestly believe you will be encouraged, challenged, comforted and blessed by the stories and encounters with God within this book.

*Christie Briers - Kings Church Salford*

# INTRODUCTION

Putting these stories together, testimonies and devotions has been a wonderful labour of love. Over the many years that I have been a Christian, meeting all of these most amazing people has been an enrichment to me.

Gleaning from others is what we do as human beings. I know how to tie my shoelaces now because I watched and listened to someone older than me who showed me how to. I know how to read my bible and conduct myself in a Christ like way through the love, patience and wisdom of many older women that God placed in my life as a new Christian.

There were a myriad of wonderful older women in the church that I first met Jesus in. My Pastor's wife Linda is an incredibly hard working and kind prayer warrior. I would sit often in the morning prayer meetings listening to Linda praying the sincerest heartfelt prayers for our town, our country and our government. Linda would also pray so sincerely for members of the congregation and her husband that it would leave me close to tears. I always wanted to be able to pray like Linda McKim. Over the years I have learned to pray like Fiona Myles.

**Nora**, my best friend and mentor, who stood by me through thick and thin. Always ready to listen and pray with me and for me. Champion cheese and mayonnaise sandwich maker too.

**Beth**, who was a powerhouse of solid no nonsense wisdom, taught me that you should just be yourself, be for real.

**Moira** is the epitome of hospitality, making things out of nothing. Getting up early to go to the markets to pick up flowers to make displays, and food to make the most amazing creations to wow her guests.

**Agnes** was the person who taught me about generosity. Often bringing dresses and jumpers to church for me as in those days, I had very little that was appropriate to wear to church.

**Margaret B**, who took me under her wing teaching me how to pray in faith for the sick and see them healed. I saw two people physically before my eyes were healed, one from smoking and one from eczema that disappeared before our very eyes.

Not forgetting the beautifully gentle **Mrs Hunter**. Bringing me onto the cleaning team at church, gently showing me the routine and the jobs that needed to be done. We met often at her house, where she would talk to me about her love for God, her failings (which I never saw) and more importantly she made me feel wanted as a person. Bear in mind I was an addict coming into this church. It amazed me that beautiful people like those mentioned above would even have me in their homes.

Honestly, our older women in all churches must be celebrated more often for the wonderful things they do behind the scenes to build new Christians and teach the beauty of servanthood.

Some of the stories are quite short, some are a bit longer. This book is meant to encourage and bless you the reader. I know and love all of the wonderful older women featured and hope that you do glean something from each person's story or short devotion.

From Freda the fantastic to Marcia the Magnificent these women are from all over the world, America, Jamaica, Scotland, Barbados, New Zealand and Bolton to name a few places.

A huge thank you to everyone who has taken the time and the effort to write a piece or two for this book. May God bless you and keep you, may He shine His face upon each one of you and your families. You are all now immortalised within the pages of this book. My prayer is that this book will encourage and help many over many years to come.

A percentage of the profit from this book will be split between The Community Grocery in Bolton and the Eden charity who work with the young women in Burma.

**To donate to either of these charities please head to**

https://communitygrocery.org.uk/donate/ To donate to the Community Grocery Bolton.

https://thisiseden.jewelry/pages/donate-1 To donate to Eden Jewellery.

# 1

# SELF-CARE IS PRAYER

I decided that I would go first. Prayer has been key in my life from the very first months of becoming a Christian, being invited to the morning prayer meetings, where I used to sit and wonder what I was doing with these praying people. I liked to listen to them all praying in different ways, some loud, some quiet, some long and some short. Listening taught me how to pray. One morning out of the blue the Pastor asked me to close in prayer, I almost fell off my chair, Me! pray out loud? Garbling something that I thought sounded like a prayer was a turning point for me. I did it. I had prayed out loud. I had of course been excellent at praying inside quietly. I still don't feel that comfortable being asked to pray out loud.

Prayer is key to our growth as Christians.

**Mark 1:35**. *"Very early in the morning, while it was still dark, Jesus got up, left the house and went off to a solitary place, where he prayed."*

As a Christian, self-care is very important to me. Especially as I grow older. It is all too easy to be caught up running around doing stuff, doing ministry, making sure everyone else is okay to the detriment of your own well-being. To be honest, neglecting yourself is dangerous especially as we grow older. When we are too busy, we can miss some pretty important signs that something is amiss.

1) We can miss signs that our body is sending us that all is not well.

2) We can become dull spiritually by just tapping into God and tapping out because we are busy.

3) We can miss those wonderful Joy bubbles that happen daily as they float over our heads in our busy states.

Each of these three things can lead to some form of death. Our physical body will die one day, but don't let that be earlier than it should have been because you were too busy to notice or deal with pain that shouldn't have been there. Spiritual death can be so easy to succumb to in our lives, thinking that we are being Spiritual by giving the people we are helping a Scripture or a learned Christian phrase. Instead of taking the time in prayer to seek a word for them.

Joy should be a daily part of our Christian menu. All too often those joy bubbles are missed never to return that day. Aim to catch tomorrow's joy bubble. Take time to look around to see the beauty in the day. The hearty laugh of a small child. A flower in bloom. The richness of the autumn hues.

Jesus got up, found a spot to be on his own and he prayed. Is that something that you do? Or are you too busy to do that? Finding your solitary spot could, in this day and age simply be standing at the sink washing the dishes. This is something I enjoy, a few minutes on my own to sing or seek God out to put some of my many thoughts, questions and fears to Him.

Prayer is most certainly an area of self-care. In the business or secular world, it can be called meditation, listening to white noise and the likes. For me the mainstay of my own self-care is making sure daily that at some point, I make that time to check my busy life out and check in with God. If you need to then schedule it into your diary.

I want to share with you one of the ways I make time with God and look after my feet at the same time. Fill a basin with warm water and add your favourite scented bubbles. Light a couple of candles, switch your phone, tablet, and television off. Dim or put the lights off, pop your feet into the water. Start to feel the water, smell the aroma from the candles and the water. Begin to engage with your creator and start to feel the wonderful peace that only comes from God.

I lead a very busy life, I am a writer, I champion adoptees and I have a child with complex needs. Becoming a parent at fifty was a shock to the system. Self-care and prayer went flying out of the window very quickly. Over time realising that the lack of self-care was affecting my parenting. Finding a completely new rhythm after Georgie arrived was hard. I had been so used to getting up with the new day, reading, praying, finding time to worship and fellowship. Suddenly mornings were not mine anymore and evenings were for recovery.

Discovering and sticking to a new prayer routine was proving difficult. I had to go rogue, praying when I could, worshipping when I could. Church was a battle ground with a baby, then a toddler. As she began to grow up, she was diagnosed with ADHD, learning difficulties and complex needs. Sunday school struggled to contain her. I spent most of my time at the back or outside church till service was finished. These wilderness years were so lonely. Covid struck in 2020 when my daughter was four. Deeper into the wilderness I roamed, wandering around looking for oasis points to stop and recalibrate spiritually. The loneliness was intense.

Prayer began to be my only solace. I needed God to move. He needed me to listen.

Eventually God moved us to a new church. Georgie loved Sunday School and settled in brilliantly. Not once did I have to leave a service because my daughter couldn't settle. She comes racing out delighted with what she has made or done. That peace alone helped me.

Prayer certainly does change things. I know only too well just how difficult it can be to maintain a strong prayer life. I have hit the snooze button many times, then wondered why life is so challenging.

I look after myself and my family now by maintaining my self-care routine which includes a daily time of reflection and prayer.

Stay on your knees in prayer or get on your knees once again to see just what amazing things God has in store for you.

**Fiona Myles age 58**
Kings Church Salford

Author of This is me - No darkness Too Deep, This is me - I'm Adopted, Adoption Trauma, Georgie Me & ADHD, and The Kings wonderful older women. All available from my website www.fionamylesauthor.com or Amazon

# 2

# TRUST IN THE LORD

Iris and her husband Laurence are a devoted, wonderful couple. Giving of themselves all the time. They have a wealth of Spiritual and life experience between them. I loved chatting with Iris. I had watched Iris over a few months, hearing her bring a devotion at a Thrive meeting. I knew that she would be perfect for this book. Listening intently as she spoke, the love that she has for the Lord shone through. It was an honour to have her onboard.

**Jeremiah 17:7-8.** *"But blessed is the one who trusts in the Lord, whose confidence is in him. They will be like a tree planted by the water that sends out its roots by the stream. It does not fear when heat comes; its leaves are always green. It has no worries in a year of drought and never fails to bear fruit."*

I was brought up in a Christian home and came to know the Lord as a young child, it was good to have that firm foundation from an early age. However, life is life and things happen, good things, bad things and tragic things. Happy times and unhappy times, all of these play a part, life will contain many twists and turns on its journey. I have been up on the mountain tops, and I have been down in the valleys, but the one thing I can say, without any doubt, is that the Lord has never left me even when I felt I was on my own.

I got married on my 17th birthday and soon found out that the man I loved had a drink problem that went on for the next 12 years, during which time I had two sons, one when I was 18 and another when I was 19. They kept me going forward over those 12 long years. I knew I needed to get closer to the Lord, so I started to attend church, taking the boys with me and starting a Sunday school, as there wasn't one at the time.

Eventually, after a lot of heartache and searching, Laurence went for help for his drink problem, and he has stuck with it and stayed sober from that day. He said that he had seen something in me and had been watching me and seeing me go to church and the difference it had made. He said that he wanted what I had and, so we asked the Pastor of my church to come and speak with him, which he did, and Laurence gave his life to the Lord that same night.

Ever since Laurence got sober and remained sober, we both began working with alcoholics and their families helping them. We were introduced to a man who had a Christian ministry to alcoholics and drug addicts. We started working with them on a voluntary basis and eventually went into full-time Christian ministry with that ministry. We did this for the next eighteen years before beginning our own ministry. We ministered for a further fifteen years until retiring.

I love the passage that I used to start my story because that tree speaks to me about my own life. I believe that as Christians, we all need to send out those roots, and soak in all that we can get from God's word, from God's people, from his church, from everything that He has given to us to feed us, to bless us and show us the way. We won't always be in the right place, or be in the right mood or be at the right point in our lives. But if we are like that tree and we send out those roots by the river, it will be stored up inside, so that when we feel dry, or we feel we can't do it today, we think we are not good enough, or we have no strength today. We can then look within, and we will find what we need for the time we are in because when we were in the good place, we soaked in the things we now need.

God knows His children and what they need. We are the apple of His eye. He says we are precious in His sight. He knows our fickle nature and our weaknesses, but He will provide, He has given us everything we need for life and for Godliness, He will never abandon us or leave us as orphans.

Now, how do we bring all this stuff up in ourselves when we don't feel we are in the right place. I find the best way is to speak back to God, all the things He has done for us in the past. In my case I can say… Are you not the God who healed me? Are you not the God who provided when I had nothing? Are you not the God who healed relationships? Take the time to make your own list, as you speak these things faith will rise in your heart, and you will feel it rising, courage and strength will come, and you will overcome all that is troubling you.

We ran a rehab in Ireland. There was no staff except Laurence and me. We had to be up first and last to bed. We did a morning devotional and an evening devotional. We prayed with people and worked in a classroom teaching them how to do life, using scripture. We oversaw the work that was done daily by the people in the rehab. It was long and tiring work, but we loved it. One day I was ironing ready to come to Bolton for a week's break, when I saw this red flashing light in neon writing in my head, flashing the word failure. Within minutes, I was saying and believing that, right, I am a failure as a Christian, a failure as a Christian wife, I'm just a big failure.

When we got to Bolton, I spent the week crying non-stop. So much so that our boss said when we returned that I was burned out. Go back to Bolton and take a couple of months of rest to recover. Do you know? I believe God allowed that to happen because He loves me and wanted to minister to me. I was in a deep valley, but He was about to lift me up. He gave me specific instructions too. He said go and buy a bible with nothing in it but my word, no notes or studies. Start to read at Matthew and read to the end but don't read the book of Revelation. Don't study it, just read it. Once you have read it all, pray, but don't ask for anything and don't pray for anybody even for yourself, just praise me and worship me. I did exactly what He said, and obedience paid off. As I prayed it felt cold like writing a letter, Dear God, but I kept going, kept praising, and as I continued in obedience, something changed inside, I felt words of praise and worship just flowing and flowing. As I read, the word became so alive. He rewarded my obedience in abundance. I was in the house alone Laurence was still running the rehab at that time. How I looked forward to that special time every morning with the Lord.

I hope that you can see through my words that life has its highs and lows, its mountains and valleys, there have been many more than these. However, if I hadn't had a valley, how would I appreciate a mountain top? God uses everything we go through if we could only see it. Sometimes we are blinded by circumstances and cannot see it, but God doesn't waste a thing. He helps us and teaches us because He wants us to be the very best that we can be. Where we see problems, He sees potential. I have something I always say to God when going through a tough time. I say, *'Lord please don't let me miss the thing you want me to learn through this experience, help me see what you are teaching me."*

Eighteen months ago, I was not in a good place, I was not happy in my Christian life, not feeling used and feeling older people are not being used to do things in church anymore. Complaining to myself and not being in the best place. God Spoke to me, He said "you started this race well, I want you to Finish it well." I was so overwhelmed that God loved me so much to care that I felt left out and feeling too old to be useful in Christian service.

As if to make sure I understood he showed me the picture of the frog that's in a pan of cold water and not noticing that the water was being heated ever so slowly that the frog didn't notice till it boiled, and it was too late. I talked with Laurence, and he was feeling the same, so we changed some things in our lives and now we are in a totally different place and mindset. Laurence is seventy-five and I am seventy-three. We both feel so young and invigorated and useful.

The Lord loves his children so much, He wants us to know how much we are loved and how much he cares. He wants the very best for us whatever age or stage of life we are at. We know more than we did when we were younger, we are wiser hopefully than when we were younger. There is no age we stop being useful to God, there is a work for Jesus, only you can do, says an old Hymn.

I hope that something here has inspired you as you read this, that being older can be an exciting part of our journey. Pray every day, "Lord I give this day to you, use me any way you can" Don't be surprised at what he sends your way, be prepared.

I'm bringing this to a close with another verse from Isaiah 46 v 4 *Even to your old age and grey hairs I am He that will sustain you. I have made you and I will carry you, I will sustain you and I will rescue you.*

**Iris Hennessey age 73**
Kings Church Bolton

# 3

# THE JOY CHALLENGE

I have to admit that I don't actually know Lisa very well. I'm happy to say I know her better now. We moved to Kings Church Salford and a few weeks later Lisa had to move on as she had moved away. During the time that we were there together I watched her fellowship and touching lives as she was going around at the Sunday services. Lisa brought a word about Joy before she left, it stuck with me that whole week. I reached out and asked if she would like to bring a word for this book. I am delighted that she said yes.

**Zephaniah 3:17** *"The LORD your God is with you, he is mighty to save. He will take great delight in you, he will quiet you with his love, he will rejoice over you with singing."*

Did you know the bible commands us to rejoice always? Even as a Christian do you sometimes find that being joyful in all circumstances is an impossible challenge?

Although I've been a Christian for over twenty years, joy as an outward manifestation of the Holy Spirit is the gift that comes the least naturally to me, I don't seem to have the same struggle with patience, kindness, or faithfulness but when it comes to joy, I would describe it as more of a dripping tap than an overflow.

Don't misunderstand me, I do experience regular moments of joy, how could I not? Twenty years ago, I was in a position that nobody would choose. Outwardly I appeared fine, but inside I was lost, and my heart was broken.

As a teenager my happy family unit had shattered into pieces overnight when my parent's relationship broke down. Angry and unable to accept my new step parents, two years later I found myself homeless until at the age of 20 I joined the military to escape my own life. But there was no running away from the feelings of rejection and for the next few years I recklessly looked for love and acceptance in all the wrong places.

Fast forward fifteen years I was a lonely single Mum of two small children, still paralysed by feelings of rejection, still feeling hopeless and isolated, practically, and emotionally life was a struggle, I was tired of my own mistakes. Thankfully over the years God had His hand on me and had placed some remarkable Christians in my world, and so alone one night having finished a book Colin Urquarts Anything You Ask that one of them had given to me, I gave in and asked Jesus into my life, it was messy and there were lots of tears as I felt His tangible presence and released the reins of my future to Him.

That night He began a transformational work in me for His glory and He has blessed me beyond measure ever since. Not only has He guided me step by step from isolation to security and from lack to abundance, but He has also given me the privilege and opportunity to share my story and His word with others.

I do hope that you too can count your blessings and see His hand at work in your life, so why is it when the inevitable storms of life invade our blessings that we can so quickly shift down a gear from joy to anxiety?

Philippians is described as the most joyful book in the bible, with the Apostle Paul using the Greek words for joy sixteen times in just four chapters. What is remarkable is that he's not writing about joy from a position of privilege he's shackled in an underground Roman prison, sharing a cell with criminals, in extreme temperatures and unsanitary conditions, reliant on others to bring food for his survival, and yet even when surrounded by every conceivable obstacle to happiness he is overflowing with real joy. In contrast our joy can start to ebb away at the first sign of stress, so how is Paul's attitude even possible? As always, we find the answer in scripture:

**Zephaniah 3:17** *"The LORD your God is with you, he is mighty to save. He will take great delight in you, he will quiet you with his love, he will rejoice over you with singing."*

Do you realise that the joy of the Lord is in YOU?

Think about that for a moment, not only were you fearfully and wonderfully made, but you are perfect in God's eyes to the point that he is delighted by you, not just some of the time but all the time. When you are facing the battles of this world and the enemy is whispering lies in your ear, when illness hits, when you are weighed down by bad news, when you are worried for others and can't figure out how to help, instead of sinking into anxiety take a moment to remind yourself that the creator God himself your ever present Father is at that very moment singing over you a song of love and delight wouldn't that make a difference?

Understanding how much he was loved and where his security came from meant that even in chains Paul had found the secret to an attitude of real joy, and we can learn to have that attitude too. Today, and everyday let's begin by reminding ourselves that we are His masterpiece, we are His delight and that His love for us is perfect.

When we do that, we will begin to release more and more of our spiritual gift of joy and be able to face any circumstance saying and believing that THE JOY OF THE LORD IS MY STRENGTH.

**Lisa Dickinson age 58**

Chief Executive Officer for Aspire, working with people who have complex learning disabilities and dementia. Lisa attends Middlewich Community Church.

# 4

# PUT YOURSELF IN THE FUTURE WITH GOD

Meeting Vanessa through an online writing course, we hit it off on two counts, we were both Christians and both had adopted children. Vanessa has been a source of encouragement to me, as she has gone before me in some of the difficulties that I am facing with my little girl. We all need people in our lives that we can relate to. The wisdom and scripture in Vanessa's piece are sure to bless you.

**Jeremiah 29:11** *"He says, "For I know the plans I have for you, declares the Lord, plans for welfare and not for evil, to give you a future and a hope."*

"Mum, I don't think I'll live beyond Christmas." My heart broke for my adopted daughter who was so incredibly sad, desperately sad. She felt that she didn't have anything to live for. Safeguarding referrals had been made and we were again seeking the help of professionals. She no longer smiled, instead preferred to stay in her bed when she was at home. What was a mother to do, for me the only thing I could do was pray. There were times though when I couldn't pray, I just cried, wept for her. It was then my friends prayed and lifted my cries. My beautiful daughter. And then one day my daughter said "Mum, next year." and I realised that I had been holding my breath all this time. But I knew and I rejoiced because she was looking forward. She had put herself in the future.

My youngest adopted daughter wasn't expected to live; and because at birth her brain didn't receive enough oxygen or blood flow for a period of time, she had HIE Grade 3, as well as other complications. (Hypoxic ischemic encephalopathy is a form of brain damage that can kill the neurons that transfer motor signals. The professionals held little hope for her future, but I knew that with God all things were possible.

Did you know that God starts with the end? Why start at the end you may ask? That's because God *always* starts with the end in mind. When He sent His Son, God knew it would end with the defeat of Satan. God knew Paul would finish the course set before him. And He sees you as you are going to be. Not as you are now.

This is The Vision that He has for you; to be perfect and complete in Him. (Colossians 2:10) And because you have been created in His image; (Genesis 1:27) the vision He has for you resides within you as well. But you may ask, does that mean that I am just the same as everyone else? Yes, we are the same, and then again, we are not. Just as snow is made up of individual flakes that are all unique; so, each and every one of us is different; and God's vision for each of us is different and unique.

The bible says, "Eye has not seen, nor ear heard, nor have entered into the heart of man, the things which God has prepared for those who love Him" (1 Corinthians 2:10). However, you will need to find out what these things are. As the scripture goes on to say, "But God has revealed them to us through His Spirit. For the Spirit searches all things, yes, the deep things of God." ...and these things have been freely given to us by God, (1 Corinthians 2:11-12)" I believe that God has formed you for a purpose and therefore you already have all the attributes that you need. But these attributes need to be revealed. Just like a diamond. A diamond is formed deep within the Earth's mantle. Under enormous pressure and immense heat, a diamond will begin to form. Then forces within the Earth bring the diamond to the surface. Yet, rough as it is, if it is a gem, it will be picked out for its value. In the same way, you have been selected because, "Everyone who is called by My name, whom I have created for My glory; I have formed him, yes, I have made him", (Isaiah 43:7).

God has made so many promises to you, you only have to read His word to find them. He says that "But if any of you lacks wisdom, let him ask of God, who gives to all liberally and without reproach, and it will be given to him.

(James 1:5) Just ask Him. You will find that His promises are not hidden from us but rather for us.

Jeremiah 29:11 He says, "For I know the plans I have for you, declares the Lord, plans for welfare and not for evil, to give you a future and a hope." One of my favourite verses of all times is Zephaniah 3:17 where it says that God rejoices over us. He looks at me and rejoices! I believe that is because He looks at us as we are going to be rather than what we are.

When we look at ourselves, we can get so disappointed, so busy looking at our circumstances, people around us, people who have gone before us. We sometimes even look at people younger than we are, seeing them with so much to live for and our lives seeming to pale in comparison. We need to stop this. We need to start believing that God has something in store for us. Something so great that it causes Him to rejoice. Isn't it wonderful to know that He knew us from our mother's womb, He knows the very hairs on our head. He loves us with such an everlasting love. (Psalm 139:13)

I remember when I first became a Christian, I had felt so unloved for most of my life, I knew my family and friends loved me, but I didn't feel love. To this day I don't know why. When I found that God loved me unconditionally it changed my whole life. To be loved without conditions attached is not something most of us are used to. And in addition, knowing that someone has a plan for us, a plan not to harm us but to prosper us, is so reassuring. To know that He has gone before us and made the crooked paths straight. (Isaiah 45:2) There is nothing He can't do.

Nothing is impossible for Him. We have it in writing, in His word. The bible says that the Spirit brings back to remembrance what we have read but if we are not reading the bible, He has nothing to bring back to us. It's as simple as that. Like we feed our physical bodies every day, we should be feeding our spiritual bodies. We need to be strong for the tasks that He has set out before us each day.

You know, we can only become what we already are, so that is how we need to see ourselves. NOT as we are now. Imagine you want to lose weight, visualising yourself as overweight, unhealthy, and fat. Even though you may well be, it will not help at all. The mind is powerful, and if we knew how powerful, there are so many things we wouldn't say, let alone think. We need to remember that we need to renew our minds daily (Romans 12:2) and that life and death is in the power of the tongue. (Proverbs 18:21). So back to visualising yourself as slim. I believe that one of the best ways is to think of yourself as a slim healthy person. Always ask yourself the question: what would a healthy person do? Would a healthy person eat three burgers and chips for breakfast? Washed down by a milkshake? No, don't think so. You would want something that is going to be healthy for your body, which after all is a temple of the living God.

Or what if you wanted to have better control of your finances, you may want to save for the future or have more money to give to good causes. Whatever the reason you need to start with a budget. Some people think that a budget only says "No, no, no." But a budget, if done correctly, will tell you what you can have.

I believe that having a vision puts you in the future with God, puts you at the end. We all have so much to give to ourselves and others. Don't let this life pass you by without you accomplishing that which you were tasked to do.

I pray that this devotion will have a big impact on your life" because, as you read it, I pray that God will reveal to you, the "You He created you to be".

**Vanessa Holmes age 63**

Mum/step mum/adoptive mum to seven children from age 52 to 6 years old.

Church Regeneration

Vanessa is a prayer warrior for her church and children.

# 5

# ABUNDANCE

Tina came into my life in January of 2015. At the time my husband and I were running a Christian Recovery Home for women through Victory Outreach. Tina was coming all the way from Australia to stay in the Home to learn the basics of how the Home was run. I remember meeting Tina on a video call first and was amazed to see her wonderful grey hair. In the months that followed Tina supported the Home and myself as my mother became very ill, culminating in many trips to Scotland to be with her till her death in August of 2015. I was exhausted managing the Home and the women in it, while managing the last few months of my mother's life emotionally. Without this Wonderful Older Woman travelling halfway around the world to do this training, I think I may have sunk without a trace. I'm beyond delighted to have Tina bring a piece for the book.

**John 10:10** *"The thief does not come except to steal and to kill and to destroy. I have come that they may have life, and that they may have it more abundantly."*

For years I only knew this verse as its first half – but the second part is the best bit! Why settle for anything but the best? We have so many examples in scripture, such as

Abraham being willing to settle for Ishmael, not realising that God had Isaac. Likewise, we need to fix our eyes on God's best for us, His abundance. Why would I aim for the wrong target when I can hit the mark?

For my life to be abundant I need abundant resources. I can be time-poor, lacking in money . . . the list goes on! The only resource that NEVER runs out is Jesus – I can NEVER come to the end of him and that's extremely reassuring. Look at all the things in the world we are manufacturing in order to be winners: weapons, cars, restaurants, yachts, palaces; I'd rather have Jesus any day. The flesh or the Spirit – every day we make that choice numerous times. Am I defeated or victorious? False gods, false celebrations, resulting in excited kids, excited adults, all absolutely misguided. We are not misled by the highs and the lows. Jesus gives us the choice: yield to God and enjoy His abundance or yield to sin and be defeated.

Romans 12:1,2 tells us to be transformed and it tells us how – to be willing to serve: "*I beseech you therefore brethren, by the mercies of God, that you present your bodies a living sacrifice, holy, acceptable to God, which is your reasonable service. And do not be conformed to this world, but be transformed by the renewing of your mind, that you may prove what is that good and acceptable and perfect will of God.*" We cannot become so well-adjusted to worldly culture that we fit in without even thinking. "Do not be conformed to this world but be transformed" is not just a casual suggestion. Even though we have the ten commandments to guide us, there is so much more that the Bible lovingly spells out for us:

"Love one another" **Jn 15:12**,

"Abide in Me" **Jn 15:14**,

"Pursue righteousness, faith, love, peace" **2Tim 2:22**,

"But the fruit of the Spirit is love, joy, peace, longsuffering, kindness, goodness, faithfulness, gentleness, self-control" **Gal 5:22, 23.**

Grace after grace after grace in chapter after chapter after chapter, exhorting us to live in the abundance of God. So,

1)  Make the choice, am I just settling for salvation or am I pursuing God's abundance?

2)  Am I willing to serve? To present my body as a living sacrifice?

To be separated from worldly ways? To take the time to seek out God's way? To pray over every circumstance? This is what builds our relationship and fellowship with God. Look at the lives of Joshua and Caleb. Everyone had been exposed to the same miracles, same grace, same mercy, same deliverance. Yet of the twelve spies and the two million Israelites, only these two were daring (full of faith) enough to claim God's promise. Numbers 14:24 tells us that they possessed a different spirit. So, if we do the maths, that makes each of them one in a million. We, too, have to be prepared to stand out, even amongst the rest of the congregation. That's the deal. Crying out over tragic situations. Hearing God's heart, Ps 143:8 *"Cause me to hear Your lovingkindness in the morning for in You do I trust. Point out the way in which I should walk – where and how – for I lift up my soul to You."* I need that every morning all day long. God's Holy Spirit. Yes, we asked to be filled with the Spirit and we are. But we might have the Holy Spirit – does He have us?

We sing "Lord, have Your way in me". Choices. In Acts 2 we know that Jesus had promised the disciples the Holy Spirit – look at the abundance that occurred when He turned up. Courage, confidence, boldness, joy. NOTHING was impossible and nothing could stop them. These disciples had made the choice, they were willing to serve, they had been obediently waiting for the Holy Spirit (Acts 1:4), and now it was like they had received their wings. The rest of the New Testament and the past 2,000 years is a testimony to the abundance they received and that we receive.

Recognising the season, being prepared/prayerful, knowing God's heart, having faith, redeeming the time

(Eph 5:16), no complacency. I will trust in You, and I will not be afraid.

**Tina Voordouw age 70**

Victory Outreach in Auckland, NZ

Principle in Primary Education, ages 5-12, Currently teaching 4 days a week.

Leading the Women's Ministry at church and serving in the Kidz Gang ministry

Love hanging out with family, tramping & knitting.

# 6

# AUTUMN OF LIFE

My dear friend Marcia has two pieces in this book. A wonderful and incredible woman who has given me the privilege of being her friend for over twenty years. Sticking by me through good times and not so good times. At one time being solely responsible for keeping a roof over our heads. As Marcia has walked through her own good and not so good times. I have watched her walk with a magnificent grace and sensitivity to the Holy Spirit.

**Psalm 23 v 1** *"The Lord is my Shepherd I shall not want."*

Autumn - my favourite season of the year. There is beauty to be found in God's creation in spring, summer and winter, but for me autumn's magnificent multi-coloured leaves make it the winner by a huge margin.

As I approached my mid-60s, I felt very much in the "autumnal" season of my life and ready to enjoy the comfortable surroundings in which I was happily planted, with my loving family and friends around me.

I had a legal career behind me of nearly 40 years but felt ready to start winding down.

I still felt passionate about representing my clients, family members of children who had come to the attention of local Authority Social Services Departments because of allegations made that they had been victims of neglect or abuse.

Seeing separated families reunited, as parents grasped new skills to ensure their children's healthy development, and parents overcoming addictions or escaping unhealthy relationships to ensure the return of their babies, involves long hours of hard work. It can be distressing and emotionally challenging but also hugely rewarding and satisfying.

Then a "chance" (or perhaps divinely inspired) phone call to a friend I'd not been in contact with since my twenties, over 40 years earlier, brought some dramatic and unexpected changes to my plans.

After I had made a few holiday visits to the Caribbean, I received an invitation to stay for a longer period, and this led to me seeking a one-year sabbatical from work.

I exchanged the streets, and family courts, of London for a small rural hamlet in the parish of St Mary, Jamaica. As I write, I am 9 months into my 12-month period of unpaid leave.

Psalm 23 reminds me that the Lord is my shepherd, and I shall not want. The Lord has indeed been faithful and sustained me through the enormous and humbling changes I have faced.

For now, there are no packed bus or train journeys to work with fellow stony-faced commuters. Instead, there are brisk morning walks at 6:00am, as 7:00am. would be too hot to take them, with 20 to 25 "Good morning" greetings along the way. They come from the young, the old and the in between. Only a few teenagers, glued to their phones as in London, sometimes fail to speak as I pass them.

There is no regular monthly income, but the Lord has provided for all of my financial and physical needs. His generosity has even allowed me to continue to bless others.

I am staying in a warm, welcoming and friendly community with a variety of houses, and households.

Some "Returnees" who have come back from living and working abroad have built elaborate mansions.

Whilst others have not travelled further than one or two parishes away from St Mary, and live in smaller more humble houses, often self-built.

Multi-generational homes are common, with many grandmothers assisting with childcare, as parents are working in the local tourist industry, on cruise ships or abroad.

Some local residents can afford, and do seek, expensive private healthcare, whilst others rely on the medical, optical and dental treatment programmes regularly provided by visiting Christian missionary associations from the USA. These are well attended, valued and appreciated, as can be seen by the fact that the queues for some clinics start forming from as early as 4am.

Mosquito bites, frequent water stoppages and unexpected power cuts, can be frustrating. As is the need to add 30 minutes to an hour to any proposed journey, as that is how long it may take before you can get a shared taxi. At such times, I would be happy to take even a crowded bus or train, but there are neither of these locally.

God has used these "inconveniences' to teach me valuable lessons in patience, being prepared and thankfulness.

The joy I feel when I open the tap with hope, and find the water is indeed back, or the bliss of getting the last space in a taxi after a long wait is indescribable.

The change of pace has allowed me to develop previously untapped gardening and cooking skills. I am loving the opportunity to be creative in these areas, and happily surprised when I receive compliments. My self-confidence has received a gigantic boost.

The Lord has also swung open doors of ministry, on a personal and wider basis. He has given me space and opportunity to exercise spiritual muscles I didn't even know I had. My life will never be the same.

On the morning of my 65th birthday recently I received an email that left me upset and anxious, followed by an unexpected invitation to climb the Dunn's River Falls in nearby Ochi Rios.

For someone who does not like heights, the thought of climbing 960 feet with water pounding fiercely against me, was daunting.

However, with the encouraging words and helping hands of supportive friends, I made it to the top of the falls and felt wonderful.

It was a highlight of my sabbatical, and physical confirmation that, when my heart is overwhelmed, the Lord will surely lead me to the rock that is higher than I, Psalm 61. I have a photograph as proof.

So let me encourage you to let the Lord lead you, in this beautiful season. There is a right time for everything, as Ecclesiastica 3 reminds us. It just may not be the time for what you had in mind, as I have found out to my joy.

So, make that call, send that message or apply for that job that has been on your mind. Who knows what the Lord has prepared in advance for you to do.

As for me, I am reminded that, as stated in Psalm 1, by delighting in the law of the Lord and meditating on it day and night, I will be like a tree planted beside water, I will bring forth fruit in its season, my leaves will not wither and whatever I do will prosper.

I haven't seen the usual beautiful array of red, orange, yellow and gold leaves this autumn. Many trees around me are still green and bearing the specific fruit that appear this time of the year. For example, avocado pears are now plentiful, rather than the mangoes of the summer months.

I long to be a fruitful evergreen tree, regardless of the physical season I am in.

Autumn is my favourite season of the year, and it looks like the autumnal season of my life may be my favourite too!

**Marcia Shields, age 65**

Family Solicitor

Shoreline Calvary Chapel North London

Worked with various Christian drug rehabilitation services. Prison chaplaincy volunteer for many years.

# 7

# WHAT IS SO GOOD ABOUT BEING AN OLDER WOMAN?

What can I say about my best friend? This wonderful older woman took me by the hand as a baby Christian, taught me about all the fundamentals while putting up with my childish behaviour. Nora is patient, kind, understanding and loving. She has four wonderful children and countless grandchildren that she loves dearly.

**Titus 2:3-5** *"Similarly teach the older women to live in a way that honours God. They must not slander others or be heavy drinkers. \*Instead, they should teach others what is good. These older women must train the younger women to love their husbands and their children, to live wisely and be pure, to work in their homes \* to do good, and to be submissive to their husbands. Then they will not bring shame on the word of God. NLT"*

In my almost thirty years as a Christian, I have had a lot of older women's input in my life, some in a mentoring capacity, others in a more friendship/fellowship role, but because of them God has given me over the years a big heart for Women, young and old!

As a child I remember always wanting a sister. I am the only girl in my family with two brothers. Our dad died when we were children, and our mum never remarried. This meant I never got the longed-for sister in my life. At thirty - six years of age I gave my life to Jesus! and realised that God was my Father, and he brought many sisters into my life with so much love and care to help me get to know Jesus better. As I was growing in my love for Jesus, he called me into counselling others through training with an organisation called Crossline. which did both face to face counselling and over the phone consultations. Those days were some of the most rewarding times of my life but also the most challenging.

Although my journey has had its difficulties including various health issues and raising four very different and individual children alongside my husband Bryan. Those years were some of the most amazing years of my life. I loved and thrived being a mother. I have had the privilege of mentoring other young women and leading them to Jesus, through counselling face to face and also over the phone. God showed me many things in that season and taught me to listen to His still small voice.

**James1:19** tells us *"Understand this, my dear brothers, and sisters: You must all be quick to listen, slow to speak, and slow to get angry."*

Just before my sixtieth birthday I moved to a new church. For the last six years I have been enjoying being fully involved within our children's ministry, hospitality, and prayer. I also serve on the team that sells Eden Jewellery. It is a charity that rescues young girls from human and sexual trafficking in Myanmar Burma. The opportunity this brings to reach other women young and old to highlight the plight of these young women and to show God's love for these girls has been truly life changing for me.

I am now officially a pensioner, it feels great. I can be classed as an OLDER Woman. I am loving this era of my life, because I love the relationships that God has brought into my life over the years. The most beautiful relationship I have now is with my Lord and saviour Jesus Christ. It has been both challenging and exciting over the years. Once I had given Him my all there was no going back. I trust Him completely. He is my love above all things.

Although I do have some health issues, I have no intention of slowing down just yet, I have just recently taken on the role of leading the women's ministry in my church. God has a great way of bringing different women of all ages and cultures together to encourage, guide, and teach each other. He delights in seeing older women being spiritual mamas to younger women.

I am immediately reminded of Elizabeth the mother of John the Baptist {"who was well along in years" Luke 1:18} when Mary went to visit Elizabeth, she must have felt overwhelmed by the news the Angel had given her, but Elizabeth knew by the holy spirit that this young woman, would be blessed among women

**Luke 1:39-45** *"A few days later Mary hurried to the hill country of Judea, to the town where Zechariah lived. She entered the house and greeted Elizabeth. At the sound of Mary's greeting Elizabeth's child leaped within her, and Elizabeth was filled with the holy spirit. Elizabeth gave a glad cry and exclaimed to Mary, "God has blessed you above all women and your child is blessed. Why am I so honoured that the mother of my Lord should visit me? When I heard your greeting, the baby in my womb jumped for joy. You are blessed because you believed that the Lord would do what he said" NLT*

How precious it must have been for Mary to know that God's favour had been acknowledged by the woman she turned to and the very fact she stayed for 3 months tells me perhaps Mary had a lot to glean from this godly older woman which she would recall throughout her pregnancy and beyond.

I too have had Godly women in my life and not all older I have been blessed with precious friends over the years some only for a season but there are those that have been constant in my life, and I wouldn't want to do life without them, we need each other and more so in these times and having godly spirit filled women around you whether they be young or old is a joy for this older woman.

We can moan about our fading youth or step up to encourage the younger women around us to find their calling and what God has for their lives.

*Father God thank you for giving me older godly women in my life who have encouraged me to be all that I can be for your kingdom please use me now that I am the older woman to encourage and mentor the younger women around me.*

*In Jesus name Amen.*

### Nora Hutcheson - Age 66
Church Vineyard Falkirk
Hospitality at Mainly Music for Mums and toddlers
Part of the Eden team helping to sell their jewellery at church and events.
Volunteering at Love Falkirk a pantry and warm space for those in need of food and friendship
Nora leads the Women's team for the women's ministry at Falkirk Vineyard

# 8

# A WOMAN OF FAITH & PRAYER

Meeting and getting to know Paula over the last few months has been incredible. Sitting at her feet so to speak and listening to wave after wave of faith filled moments in her life has been fantastic. Paula could write a book of her own. Trying in this piece to condense Paula's incredible journey was difficult. Through an amazing faith filled relationship with God Paula has carried herself beautifully through so much in life.

**Romans 8 v 28** *And we know that in all things God works for the good of those who love him, who[a] have been called according to his purpose.*

My bible was at the side of my bed. My mastectomy was booked for the next day. I had peace about the whole situation. A nurse came in to do my observations and, spying the Bible, asked if I was a Christian. She was also a Christian which gave me some comfort to know. I could see that the lady in the bed next to me was listening to our conversation. I knew God was going to be moving in our ward over the next few days. My son had been in to visit; he has not really been open to me talking to him about my faith. As I was settling into my bed the hospital chaplain came into the ward to pray with the lady next to me, my son left the ward to head home for the night and I prayed with the lady as well.

After she had been prayed for, I stayed to talk to her. She expressed that she had 'felt' something. I explained to her that it would have been the Holy Spirit she had felt. I found a bible in one of the other bedside cabinets for her as she said she had never read a bible before. She asked where to start, I pointed her to the book of John as a good starting point.

That evening a young lady came on to the ward, she had suffered a miscarriage. She was very upset. I went over to comfort her; she was also a Christian. The next day my son visited me, and I introduced him to the couple who had lost their baby. The husband testified to my son. I was delighted to hear it. God was surely moving. It can sometimes be in the most difficult of times that God moves in spectacular fashion. Here I was with breast cancer awaiting a mastectomy, hearing my son being testified to and guiding someone to read a bible. Thankfully the cancer had not spread, and my lymph nodes were clear.

Going back a bit in time, I have a degenerative disorder called CMT which is Charcot - Marie - Tooth syndrome. From the ages of three to fifteen I was a dancer which helped with the CMT symptoms. My two son's Sean and Tony both inherited the same disorder. With CMT I can suffer from chronic fatigue. I have to be very careful how I plan each day, especially as I have grown older. Should I do too much in one day it can knock me for six for the next couple of days, so staying in a good balance with my time and energy are essential to my well-being.

Sadly, in two thousand and twelve my son Sean tragically took his own life, his battle with the symptoms and difficulties that CMT sufferers can have, completely overwhelmed him.

At fifteen years of age, I started work in an office doing admin. I got married but unfortunately my marriage was abusive, after seven years in that abusive marriage, I moved away to Whitby to remove myself and my boys from the situation. After a season of being away we moved back to where we had lived before, and I got on with my life.

I was given the opportunity to train as a hairdresser at forty years of age after an aunt left me some money. I loved being a hairdresser and met many interesting people. During my time as a hairdresser, I met a client who was a Christian. She spoke to me about her faith and taught me things from the bible. During this time, I had a vision of Christ in my home. I knew a sensation went from my feet to my head and believed this overwhelming sense that I was loved. I have followed Christ from then to now. Growing in that love. God has an appointed time for us all to come to Him.

Over many years of enduring so much in my life I have come to realise that God has used both chronic and emotional pain as a chisel in my life, as He creates His masterpiece.

As I look back over the last thirty years of walking with God, I can see how walking in obedience to Him as I faced major challenges, for example, breast cancer and the death of my son, plus let's not forget the smaller challenges that we all face in life every day. The Lord has used these times to deepen my faith and reveal more to me of who He is. I in turn have grown to love Him more, because of His faithfulness. As I look back over the last few years having the privilege of time to spend with Him. It has been a source of enrichment to me to be at His feet listening. I have come to understand that faith, hope and love are the keys we need, as the bible tells us that. If we avail ourselves of His love then the Holy Spirit can work through us and shine His light not because of who we are, but because of who He is. Simply put, God is love.

**Paula Williams - age 80**

Church - Kings Church Salford

Paula serves whenever she can in the hospitality ministry.
Paula is also a mighty prayer warrior.

# 9

# GOD IN ALL HIS MAGNIFICENCE

**Matthew 11:28-30**. *"...Come to me, all you who are weary and burdened, and I will give you rest. Take my yoke upon you and learn from me, for I am gentle and humble in heart, and you will find rest for your souls. For my yoke is easy and my burden is light."*

Throughout my life I have managed a few health issues. Warned that I could die if I didn't stop taking drugs and alcohol. Operations as a child and invasive infertility treatment for years. Eventually having a full hysterectomy at fifty-two, as there was a pre-cancerous tumour in my womb. The bombshell of having such a huge operation lasted for nearly four years. Fluctuating between being grateful that I had been infertile and never given birth naturally which meant that I couldn't have keyhole surgery. And being angry that I had gone through such a huge procedure leaving a scar from one side of my body to the next. Realising that if I had been able to have children I may not be here today as a small part of my bowel was attached to my womb, which would not have been noticed with keyhole surgery.

God in all of His magnificence did not answer my cries, my wails, my pleadings for a child because He knew that day was coming. I became a Mum at fifty after waiting thirty-three years for a child of my own. Losing a baby boy at twenty weeks through being beaten half to death by my partner at the time. Also losing twins conceived through IVF early on in their conception. Thinking always about why? Why God? Brian and I would make great parents. He knew we would, but He also knew that His timing and His plan would be perfect for us.

At a huge conference in twenty fourteen I remember very clearly God calling me to the altar. I really struggle in crowds. I get overwhelmed with people and noise very quickly. I didn't want to make my way through thousands of bodies to the front. Eventually I arrived right at the front. It didn't feel too bad as I could only see the stage in front of me, but my heart was pounding at the monumental effort it had taken to get to that point. I began to worship and ask God what do you want me here for?

He told me, "you will have a child at fifty" It felt to me that everything went silent for a few seconds. I was left holding this knowledge in my heart. Then the questions started. How? Why fifty? Where?

A tap on the shoulder pulled me from the moment. I got on with looking after the women that I had brought to the conference. I said nothing about it to anyone then put a fleece out about whether to share my word or not. I was asked to share about my time at the conference by the Pastor the Sunday that we all arrived back in the UK. I recall coming down from the stage thinking "Well, it's over to you now God".

In the January of twenty seventeen which was six weeks before my fifty first birthday God placed my daughter Georgie into our care. Our child was here, the one we had been promised. The first few weeks were bliss, then the reality of being an older parent set in. My body didn't like it, my spiritual life went up in smoke and my marriage became lukewarm.

Georgie's needs were huge, she had medication to take for seizures, she was allergic to multiple things which caused untold amounts of drama often. Always being vigilant is tiring. Being afraid to get things wrong is tiring. Arguing about the best practice for our daughter was tiring. Watching her during the night in case she had a seizure or worse was tiring.

It took a long time to get the balance back into my prayer life. Then work had to start on our marriage. We realised quite quickly that no one was at fault for where our marriage was at. Except ourselves! We had poured so much into making sure we were the best parents we could be to Georgie, alongside five very close friends passing away, both of us dealing with major life changing surgery and a host of other smaller life issues. We had not had any focus on ourselves as individuals or as a couple.

As the penny dropped as to how to change the state of our marriage, we began to make sure we took time away from Georgie and each other, pursued our own dreams again and became closer than ever in the process. God began to shine His light into our relationship in a new way.

God is good all the time. He loves us unconditionally. He wants us to succeed and keep going forward. We knew that although we had not gone back into our old lives of addiction etc. We were stagnant, only just staying clear of becoming stinky by treading water. It took effort from us both to regain a flow of the Holy Spirit once again in our marriage and other relationships.

God says Come to me all of you that are heavy laden. So why do we not do that? We didn't for such a long time. Why? All I can tell you is that we were blind to what was going on because all we could see was our daughter and her needs. Covid hit in the midst of the mess. We became very isolated and lonely too.

As the church began to meet again, we really struggled to find our feet in it. Everything seemed alien to us for some reason. After a lot of soul-searching prayer and many tears we decided to leave after almost twenty years of being a huge part of our church. Joining a new church was difficult for me to say the least. Being in a very low place Spiritually, physically and emotionally, I struggled to lift my head.

As God ministered in His gentle, humble way, and mature, gentle and humble leaders reached out to me. God began to lift my head again, removing the heaviness as I put on once again the garment of praise that had somehow dropped to the floor in my time of misery.

Are you heavily burdened by the cares of this life? My word for you is - *Lift up your head my child as I look upon you, I shine my love towards you, feel the warmth of my love begin to fill you once again. I will never leave you or forsake you my dear child. You are the apple of my eye. Come forth from your tomb and live again.*

**Fiona Myles 58**

Kings Church Salford

Author of five books

This is Me - No Darkness Too Deep,

This is Me - I'm Adopted, Adoption Trauma, Georgie Me & ADHD, The Kings Wonderful Older Women.

Available from my website www.fionamylesauthor.com or Amazon.

# 10

# GOD SURPRISES AN OLDER WOMAN

I have known Lydia for many years, my first thought about this incredible lady are her powerful gifts in evangelism and prayer. She is steadfast and immovable, an example to many. Spreading the word and truth are important to Lydia. There are many who will be making their way to heaven through her wonderful ministry and love. A wonderfully wise older woman, God uses in a mighty way.

**Luke 1: 25** *"The Lord has done this for me. In these days he has shown his favour and taken away my disgrace among the people".*

The story of Elisabeth, the mother of John the Baptist in the first chapter of Luke's gospel, is my favourite story found in the bible about God's choice of older women in His plans. Elisabeth was descended from Aaron and his priestly line and her life was in public view as she was married to a priest in Israel. Her role doubtless would have been one of leadership to support/encourage younger women in their lives and faith. When we meet Elisabeth, she is old and has been barren all her married life living with the unfulfilled desire for her own family and being reminded of this as she ministered to young women and their growing families.

In addition to the absence of the sound of joyful children in her own home she also carried the daily stigma of being barren. Yet, despite the pain she endured and the unanswered questions she must have had, she continued to love and serve her Lord. Her relationship with GOD was not in jeopardy because she did not get her heart's desire. She continued to keep the first commandment - "You shall have no other gods before me" (Exodus 20:3). She did not put the god of family before her love for GOD. She continued to love the Lord her GOD with all her heart, mind, soul and strength. That is not to say, however, that she did not question GOD or experience pain.

She knew GOD could do miracles, she would have known about her ancestor Sarah and her husband Abraham who had a child in their old age but the miracle had not happened for her and her husband Zechariah. But Elisabeth was a "righteous" woman who, despite the challenge of being barren and the many questions and tearful prayers she must have uttered in private, remained faithful serving her Lord for many years.

By GOD's sovereign choice and timing, Zechariah was visited by an angel from the presence of GOD, promising them a child telling him that their prayers had been heard.

Elisabeth acted in faith and engaged in sexual activity with her husband on his return from duty at the temple. As a consequence of her faith she received the promise and became pregnant. Elisabeth said, *"The Lord has done this for me. In these days he has shown his favour and taken away my disgrace among the people".* **Luke 1: 25**.

On becoming pregnant Elisabeth went into seclusion and I feel sure this was a time for her to draw closer to her GOD, entering His presence with great thanksgiving, rejoicing over answered prayer and expectation of GOD's word being fulfilled *"he will be a joy and delight to you".* **Luke 1:14.**

The Holy Spirit had rejuvenated both Zechariah and Elisabeth's reproductive organs to produce a son, whom Jesus described as "the greatest of all prophets". The angel Gabriel described the role of the promised child in great detail *"he will be great in the sight of the Lord…. Many of the people of Israel will he bring back to the Lord their GOD. And he will go on in the spirit and power of Elijah, to turn the hearts of the fathers to their children and the disobedient to the wisdom of the righteous - to make ready a people prepared for the Lord".*
Luke 1: 14-17.

Elisabeth and Zechariah were certainly rewarded for their faithfulness and given the very high honour of bringing up the one Isaiah and Malachi the prophets had said would come to *"prepare the way"* before the Lord. **Malachi 3:1 Isaiah 40:3-5**.

The time of seclusion would surely also have been necessary as Elisabeth was being prepared for another surprise role GOD had saved up for her old age. In the sixth month of Elisabeth's pregnancy we hear of the angel Gabriel making another appearance on earth. This time visiting a young virgin girl giving her the astounding news that she would have a baby without engaging in sexual activity.

This was an even more challenging promise than Elisabeth had dealt with. Gabriel used Elisabeth's miracle to encourage Mary that *"nothing is impossible with GOD"*. **Luke 1: 37**. As shocked as Mary was, she agreed to GODs will saying *"I am the Lord's servant. May it be to me as you have said"* **Luke 1: 38**. Elisabeth was well placed to assist Mary through this challenge as she herself had encountered the power of the Holy Spirit in her own womb despite the impossibility of her situation.

The same Holy Spirit would now come upon Mary as the power of the Most High would overshadow her so the Holy One to be born would be called *'the Son of GOD'* **Luke 1: 35**. How could Mary tell anyone what was happening to her? No one would believe her. The two women were relatives but lived many miles apart. Mary lived in the north of the country in Galilee whilst

Elisabeth lived in the south of the country in Judea. They may have only seen each other once a year in Jerusalem at a national festival possibly.

However, GOD knew that Mary needed the spiritual and practical support of a godly older woman and through the angel's words Elisabeth was highlighted to Mary as a relationship she needed to pursue. Mary was obedient and *"got ready and hurried to a town in the hill country of Judea, where she entered Zechariah's home and greeted Elisabeth"*. **Luke 1: 39-40.**

Mary was perhaps very anxious about how she would tell her relative her incredible news and what reaction she would receive. But Elisabeth was a godly woman and sensitive to the Holy Spirit. On Mary's arrival before they even had time to catch up on news, Elisabeth had confirmation of what Mary was about to disclose to her as she was filled with the Holy Spirit and *"in a loud voice she exclaimed: Blessed are you among women and blessed is the child you will bear. But why am I so favoured that the mother of my Lord should come to me?....Blessed is she who has believed that what the Lord has said to her will be accomplished"*. **Luke 1: 41-45.**

How relieved must Mary have been to hear those words. The women were walking a similar journey and knew this relationship had been provided by GOD for His purposes in their lives. I'm sure their relationship deepened considerably as they shared their journeys in the next three months. Whilst Elisabeth would never have encountered any woman having become pregnant without sexual intimacy, she had walked faithfully with GOD for many years and her maturity of faith and her own powerful encounter of the Holy Spirit's power, prepared her to support Mary facing a very unusual task.

Mary, a young woman in her faith and life experience, may have been afraid of the task ahead of her, despite her obedience and faith. She likely had many questions and had never encountered the supernatural realm before. She would also be undergoing many changes in her body and emotions in the first trimester of pregnancy that Elisabeth would already have passed through.

Mary had been given a role that no other person on earth had ever done and GOD knew she would need support to cope with this assignment. Her own natural mother would probably have struggled to support Mary given the exceptional circumstances. However, The Lord provided a place of understanding, privacy and love for Mary during the period of seclusion. Elisabeth, as the wife of a priest, would have counselled many other young women getting married and going through pregnancy. She had a capacity to love and nurture younger women that Mary needed.

Besides practical chores Mary could help Elisabeth within her sixth month of pregnancy, doubtless the two women spent time praying together and worshipping their Lord gaining spiritual strength from the time spent in His presence.

Long conversations would have taken place including perhaps talking about how Mary would face the people on her return to Galilee as a pregnant woman. Elisabeth's past experience of enduring the pain of being looked down on for being childless, in a civilisation where women were defined by motherhood, would now be drawn on to help Mary who would be accused of carrying an illegitimate child.

This is a wonderful example of how GOD is able to turn our pain into a blessing for others.

**1 Corinthians1:4** *"God comforts us in all our troubles, so that we can comfort those in any trouble with the comfort we ourselves have received from GOD"*.

Elisabeth's experience of the wonderful power of the Holy Spirit in her life, along with years of walking with the Lord through varied seasons of life, made her an ideal "spiritual mother" giving support to Mary going through a very bewildering time in her life. Elisabeth too would have received much in return as well, from the young woman of faith preparing to give birth to the Saviour of the world.

*Elisabeth was surprised by the unlimited power of GOD and received a great blessing in her older years.*

After walking with Jesus for over forty years I know GOD is able to surprise us even when we have experienced His Power and Provision in many ways through the changing seasons of our lives.

He always has something more and is a very creative and loving Father. I have found great joy and fulfilment in discipling many and received much in return. There is a great need for younger women to have role models who will stand alongside them praying and supporting whilst they step out in faith to follow the call of God in their lives.

*Who are you supporting/discipling in the ways of GOD? I encourage you to pray and ask the Holy Spirit to connect you with those people He has assigned for you to support.*

## Lydia Smith - Age 55-65
Victory Outreach Manchester
Lydia has her own ministry incorporating a regular bible fellowship group for bible study and pastoral care, evangelism training and support. She also works with Manchester Gospel Fest- open air outreach in partnership with local churches and ministries. And conducts interviews to showcase what God is doing.

# 11

# TRUST IN THE LORD
## THROUGH THE TOUGH TIMES

Ann and I came to Kings Church Salford around the same time, it was nice to have another newbie to talk to. It can be hard trying to fit into a new church and make friends. Ann's son Paul is in a writing group, so a great connection was made. Listening to Ann speak about her life at an event we both attended I just knew she needed to get her story into the book. I'm happy to say she agreed.

**Proverbs 3 v 5** *"Trust in the Lord and lean not on your own understanding."*

At the moment as I write this piece, I'm sitting in my flat looking out of the window watching the leaves fall off the trees wondering at how the leaves change colour before they fall. This makes me think about how God has always been there when I have fallen.

Born and bred in Salford to a very caring mum and dad. We never had a lot of money, but we always had clothes on our backs and food on the table. Our home was always welcoming and warm, where our friends were always made to feel welcome too.

I moved out to get married, but unfortunately my first marriage broke down, Mum and Dad welcomed me back home with open arms. I stayed at home for another six years working as a conductor on the buses. When I met Alan, my dad was never happy with him, always saying, "He's not right for you". After a few black eyes and a lot of prayer I finally had the strength to end it with him. I thank my dad for being so straight with me.

Around six months later our neighbour's son Jim asked me out, I hadn't really known him well, I had known his brothers better. We went out steadily for two years before we were married. We bought a lovely home of our own in Seedley. I had a steady job working 8am to 5pm, Jim worked at Pilkington's tiles doing shift work.

As I had been married before and had not fallen pregnant, I began to wonder if having a child was not going to be for us. I knew that Jim would have loved to have children. Even though at this point in my life I was not attending a church, I kept praying about it. I brought to mind a scripture from the bible that said Trust in the Lord with all your heart, lean not on your own understanding from Proverbs 3 v 5.

Jim and I had been married for just over a year when I was able to give him the good news that we were going to be parents. It was time to get the house in order. We had a baby on the way. As Jim was decorating one of the rooms, he fell off his ladder, he insisted that he was alright.

Our son Paul was born safe and sound, we were delighted to be parents, all was going well until Jim began to suffer with pain in his back. After much investigation, we were given the devastating news that Jim had lung cancer. Everything happened very quickly after that. Jim was under Christie's hospital receiving full treatment. I can remember the doctors telling myself and Jim's brother Bill that Jim may only have six weeks to live. When Jim was given the news, his words were "No! I will see my son grow up".

I asked the hospital if Jim could come home, Paul was only twelve weeks old. They agreed but he could only stay in the living room downstairs as he had no feeling in his legs after the treatment. Two years later, after some very frightening times with his health, I was washing his legs and he exclaimed Ann don't press too hard. I realised then that the feeling was coming back into his legs.

Getting in touch with Jim's consultant, he came out to the house to check out what was going on. He prescribed some strong physiotherapy which they agreed to do in the house. After a year of physiotherapy, we decided that a bungalow would suit our needs better. Unable to get a mortgage on a bungalow we were offered an adapted bungalow in Little Hulton. This meant that we were away from our families who had been a fantastic help to us.

Our lives began to get better. Paul was growing up and getting involved in the Scouts, Swimming, St John ambulance groups and Amateur dramatics, which we became involved in too. Looking back over these years as I sit here, I realise just how much God did see us through these years. Even though Jim was in a wheelchair we all led busy fulfilling lives. Psalm 23 always encouraged me.

Paul was now seventeen years old, growing up into a happy healthy young man. He was doing one of the Duke of Edinburgh Awards when he went off hiking in the Yorkshire dales in the cold month of November. When he came home, he was not himself, very quiet and withdrawn. He had a bath and went to his bed. This went on for a couple of days, not speaking and staying in his bed. I called the doctor in; he sent him off to the Children's hospital where he stayed for a month. We never really got to the bottom of what happened to Paul on that hike. It was over nine months later that Paul told us that he had been attacked.

Paul was still not himself, but we went on our holiday for the disabled anyway. I was very concerned about Paul, he was alright travelling to Westen super mare but the next day in the dining room he has a grand mal seizure, he had never had seizures before. Jim stayed at the hotel with our friends while I took Paul to the hospital. As Paul lay on the bed the staff were buzzing around doing all sorts of tests. Once they had left us alone, I put my hands on Paul and began to pray. As I prayed a mist fell around the bed everything went very quiet, a beam of light moved over Paul from his head to his feet ending with a light noise.

Opening his eyes as the light moved away Paul said, "Are you alright mum?" I knew that he was going to be okay. A short time later a nurse arrived to let us know that Paul was not going to need to be admitted, but advised to get to our own doctors when we got home. Arriving back at our chalet, I started to tell Jim what had happened at the hospital, as it turned out Jim was praying for Paul at exactly the same time as I had been.

Over the years we have had battle after battle with the doctors and medical profession about Paul's health. As a mother I knew my son was struggling, but no one would listen to me. On our return from Weston Super Mare, we were guided into a wonderful Christian Church. I thank God as I think back and realise just how much my faith and the strength God has given has brought me through so much.

My darling Jim died in 2007. He lived for twenty-eight years after his six weeks left to live diagnosis. We had been married for thirty years. Paul had a huge breakdown after his dad died. Life has not been easy. God is carrying us through. We still live good busy lives with the odd health issue going on.

There are two songs that never fail to lift my spirit One day at a time sweet Jesus and Be still for the presence of the Lord is moving all around. My spirit is lifted as I watch the leaves fall from the trees and know that God has us in the palm of His hand. That moment in the hospital will never leave me. I know who holds my future.

**Ann Hallows age 78**

Kings church Salford

Part of the Blend Cafe team

# 12

# ENLARGE YOUR TERRITORY

My friend Erika hails from South Africa, living in London now. Is there anything that Erika can't do? Building websites, helping people in business, being a wife and mother while working at her local doctor's surgery. Where she found the time to put together this brilliant piece, I just don't know. I am so grateful for all the support Erika has given me over the last few years.

**1 Chronicles 4:9-10** *"Jabez was more honourable than his brothers. His mother had named him Jabez, saying, 'I gave birth to him in pain.' Jabez cried out to the God of Israel, 'Oh, that you would bless me and enlarge my territory! Let your hand be with me and keep me from harm so that I will be free from pain.' And God granted his request."*

"Bless, bless me God, bless me richly".

The first time I heard the song about Jabez's prayer it deeply touched me. It also caused me to ask myself some questions.

May we ask God to enlarge our territory? May I, as a Christian woman, ask to be blessed and blessed in the business world. Is it not like asking for earthly wealth? Is it not greedy?" Pondering over these questions I began to look more closely at the scripture.

The name Jabez is of Hebrew origin and appears in the Old Testament of the Bible.

It is derived from the Hebrew word "yabetz" which means "he will cause pain" or "he makes sorrowful".

In 1 Chronicles 4:9-10, Jabez is noted for his earnest prayer to God to bless him and enlarge his territory, contrasting with the meaning of his name.

Is my territory the clients that I serve? When I ask, 'enlarge my territory,' I'm not asking God to let me enlarge my territory, but rather that He brings the right people across my path that He wants me to work with or help.

When I was much younger (in my twenties) I wrote this poem:

*Sometimes I wish I were a tree,*

*Plucking flowers to give freely.*

*To each who walks along my way,*

*A touch of love and friendship may stay.*

*Yet it's a lesson tough to discern,*

*That God decides to whom my blooms will turn.*

Sometimes we see that things that happened 30 years apart can be connected. So, the poem I wrote when I was twenty and Jabez's prayer gives me the same message. I must remain available and believe that God will determine who my clients are. I just need to be ready to use my talents and gifts where He guides me.

I have to confess that I have occasionally taken on clients with whom I've felt uneasy from the outset. It poses a significant challenge when you're tasked with creating a website and collaborating closely with a client, especially when you find yourself at odds with their message or product. The instinctive reaction might be to decline the opportunity; however, there have been instances where, even after prayerful consideration, I've accepted and later understood that there was a purpose behind it. As my dear friend Anne often says, events aren't mere coincidences but "God-incidences"—there's a reason behind them.

So, you may wonder, do I see myself as the quintessential businesswoman? Far from it. I make numerous mistakes, poor choices, and don't generate as much revenue as I'd like. I both cause and experience disappointments and sometimes overextend myself. I am very much a work in progress, whether it's in growing in my faith, nurturing relationships, or any other facet of my life. However, I am learning to place my trust in God, rather than in people or even myself.

In business planning you are often asked what your mission and vision is for your company/business. I for one, cannot say that I have the answer. I am constantly learning and evolving, I am always amazed at where God leads me. I would start following and learning from an expert and then find out that they are a Christian too, and that I can learn so much more than business and technical skills from them. That is what happens if I trust that God will show me the way, that it is not a fight for survival, that it is not important for me to know the answers. That I should trust the God behind the people, not the people.

The Jabez prayer serves as my business motto now in my 50s. It emphasises the importance of being open and prepared for the opportunities that may come my way. I believe that with God's guidance, I will be able to serve the right people using my talents and gifts. Making an income is of course important to me, but serving my clients well, allows them to have the best service. Thus, producing a lasting testimony of a Christian businesswoman.

*'Oh, that you would bless me and enlarge my territory!*

**Erika Beumer age 55+**

Church SA congregation

Website www.erikabeumer.com

Author of Your Website Your Way

# 13

# GOD BROUGHT ME 'EDEN'

Meeting Heather at Falkirk Vineyard Church has been such a blessing. I listened as she passionately talked about her ministry with Eden. Brought to tears about the plight of these young girls, I wanted to know more and wanted to support Heather in what she is doing. Having Heather write a piece for this book seemed like a no brainer. I bravely asked her if she would like to get involved. Heather has written a lovely piece for us. A percentage of all sales of this book will be going to Eden to help the work they are doing.

**Isaiah 1 v 17** "*Learn to do right, seek justice. Defend the oppressed. Take up the cause of the Fatherless, plead the cause of the widow.*"

I head up the UK side of an amazing organisation called 'Eden' which rescues young girls from human trafficking. I want to encourage all of you more mature ladies with my story of how God has used me.

I needed something new in my life, through circum-stances that happened to me about ten years ago. God asked me to leave where I was and to 'be still'. So, for a few years, I did this by going to a new church. Then one day, at work, a girl said to me, "There is a new church in Falkirk, and you need to go to it!"

I thought, 'Why not?' As it is closer to my home, that Sunday, I went along. I walked in and the first thing I saw was beautiful jewellery on sale. I approached the table and heard about 'Eden'. I knew in my heart right away that I wanted to be involved with it! After a few weeks, I approached the team and asked if I could help. So, one Sunday a month with a small table, I helped sell and promote 'Eden' at church.

After a while, the lady who was heading our team was standing down, so we all prayed about who would be the best person to take this on. In my heart, I knew I wanted to do this, but I waited to hear what everyone had to say after we had all prayed and, to my surprise, they all agreed that I should take it on.

I found this very daunting, as it was so much more than I thought. I got to learn more about 'Eden' and their work and, as time went on, I felt more and more love for the young girls involved. I couldn't understand how I could love them so much, as I hadn't met any of them. This is what God's love is like.

As time went on, I wanted to do more to help, and I got more involved with 'Eden'. Well, before I knew it, I was asked if I wanted to head up the UK side! How did that happen? I am still trying to figure that out.

You have to know that I am the most unlikely person to be doing this and it is so far out of my comfort zone. I am now sixty-one and I was thinking, 'God, it's time for me to be winding down.' But God had other ideas for me, and He was saying, 'No, Heather, I have work for you to do.' I was saying, 'Please ask someone else!' But God only wants our YES, so I had to be obedient.

God has opened so many doors for me and He has brought the right people alongside. Even

down to all the events that we have taken 'Eden' jewellery along to, He has brought them to me.

I am the most technophobic person that you will ever meet, and it scares the life out of me being of the older generation. But God has brought younger girls with that gift to me. Praise God! What I am trying to say is that, if God asks you to do something, He will equip you to do it.

We got the chance to go to Myanmar in Burma just before lockdown. I went over with my friend Sandra to see first-hand the work that 'Eden' was doing, and it was life-changing for me to actually meet some of those beautiful girls.

I will never forget the moment that we first met them. We were so excited and nervous, all at the same time. When the doors opened, they all came running towards us for a hug. It took my breath away. We sat down on a sofa and were surrounded by the girls, who were fanning us. I said, "God, this is not how I wanted it to be." I had gone over there to serve them!

The love we felt from those girls was overwhelming and I had never before experienced how people, who have nothing, can give you everything. It was very humbling and life changing.

One of the first things that these girls get taught, after lots of trauma counselling, is how to put together beautiful jewellery. They have a jewellery designer who sits down with them and listens to their story. Each piece is then designed around that girl's individual story so, when you buy the piece of jewellery, you also have a beautiful story.

I like to say that it is 'jewellery with a purpose' as, by buying it, you are supporting these girls. Every penny goes to 'Eden' to give the girls a wage and to further the work that is being done. By wearing the jewellery, you can tell people about it, and you are raising awareness about human trafficking.

'Eden' then empowers the girls by asking what their dream is; if they want to be a beautician, hairdresser, seamstress or work with computers, etc. They are then trained to do this so that, when they leave the programme, they can open a shop, get a job or work from home and be able to support themselves and their families.

This is only a small part of what the 'Eden' organisation does. Their services include prevention programmes, counselling, health support, outreach, safe houses, vocational training and economic empowerment.

There is an online shop on www.thisiseden.org where you can buy the jewellery and read the incredible stories of these girls, my heroes, in the wonderful online magazine.

I am still trying to figure out how I got to where I am. It is such an honour and a privilege to be a small cog in the wheels of justice, trying to end human trafficking.

**Isaiah 1:17** "Seek justice. Help the oppressed. Defend the cause of the orphans. Fight for the rights of the widow."

This was a verse that God had put on my heart before I became involved with 'Eden' and, at the time, I didn't understand why. But God knew, and I just had to say YES! I want to encourage you that, no matter what age you are, God has a plan and a purpose for your life.

I started, one Sunday a month, helping out with 'Eden' and am now heading up the UK side for them, just by saying YES!

We have all been given gifts by God and, by praying into these gifts, God will show you what He has for you. Just be ready for it NOT to be what you expect! With God, there is always more.

**Proverbs 20:29** *"The glory of the young girl is their strength. The grey hair of experience is the splendour of the old."*

We have life experience and God will use this for His glory. We only have to say YES! If God can do this with me, He can do it with you.

My prayer is that you will lean into what He has for you. Step out of your box and wait and see what the Lord will do.

**Heather Cunningham age 61**

Falkirk Vineyard Church

Eden - www.thisiseden.org visit to buy some of the beautiful jewellery the girls have made.

# 14

## THE POWER OF FRIENDSHIP

Freda was one of the first people I saw on the welcome at Kings Church Bolton. Having left my previous church after twenty years it felt really daunting to start again in a new church. Her smile and warmth were comforting. After a couple of weeks, I had a need for prayer as I didn't want to stay. Freda was brilliant, talking me through it and more importantly listening to me. She invited me to Thrive for the over fifty fives. I loved it, I felt so welcome, everyone was so friendly. Freda has a gift; she is wonderful at making you feel a part of things.

**Jeremiah 29 v 11** *"For I know the plans I have for you," declares the LORD, "plans to prosper you and not to harm you, plans to give you hope and a future."*

No matter our beginnings or difficulties in life, God always has a plan for us. I am prospering in my life with Him as I continually follow Him and stay on the path that He has for me.

My Mum was conceived outside of marriage which resulted in my grandma being sent off to America to stay with her sister as it was very much frowned upon in those days to have a child outside of wedlock. While she was in

America my grandma had another illegitimate child. When my Mum was fourteen, she was brought back to England as my grandma was very homesick.

My mum was sent to the Mills to work, being teased mercilessly for being a yank. Mum married and had three girls. I had an older sister who was bossy, and a younger sister who I was very close to. My older sister started being unwell, having difficulties walking and other symptoms. Ending up being bedridden. Her husband left her, and she was then put into a care home. Eventually it was said that she had multiple sclerosis. My sister died in her forties.

My sister Sheila and I took her out to listen to a visiting preacher in Bolton Town Hall where she gave her heart to the Lord. This gives me great comfort to know that she is safely with the Lord and able to skip and dance with no pain. We will see her again one day.

My Mum and Dad brought us up to be respectful and behave in a godly manner, even though we didn't go to church. We couldn't go to church as we had no Sunday clothes to attend. I do remember my sister asking for a bible for Christmas which she got.

My Dad was one of seven, he was the middle of three brothers, his mother had suffered with epilepsy, she had a seizure clearing out the fire one day, she died from that seizure being found in the hearth. His dad remarried to a woman who wasn't as kind as his mum had been. As an example, my dad worked in the Mill with a Spinner. The mums would come down with a sandwich for lunch, but his step mum never came with anything. The spinner noticed this and brought him some lunch. He was a very hardworking man who wouldn't allow my mum to work in the beginning, but then he relented and allowed her to work. This allowed us to have good shoes and holidays. My dad was a good man, but a man's man not given to showing much affection.

My Mum had a hole in her heart. In her late thirties she had a massive stroke that she recovered well from. Apart from her right arm which would hang at the side of her. She died at forty-six from pneumonia.

My husband Derek and I were married fairly young. We had three children. My parents had brought us up with a healthy respect for God. But I can't say that I actually knew Him in my younger years, but we did attend Sunday school.

As life went on, we had a fairly normal kind of family lifestyle. Life was steady and good. I remember one Easter watching the film Jesus of Nazareth. The trial of Jesus and the scourging brought me to tears. I knew that I wanted to start going back to church. My sister joined me, and we began going to a local church nearby. We enjoyed going, but there came a point where we wanted to move. We found another local church where the new vicar was born again.

We were all confirmed as a family into the church. The classes that we attended were just like the Alpha classes that we see today. I was fully involved with the church and sat on the church council. I made many good friends over the years.

Throughout my time growing as a Christian, I had a wonderful mentor called Jean. Friendships are very important to me especially in my Christian walk.

Unfortunately, my husband Derek had a heart attack at the age of thirty-nine. It was a shock, but he recovered well, and life continued. Prayer was important to me at that time. People prayed for us through this tough time. He was then diagnosed with lung cancer. Again, the power of prayer came into play as his tumour was gone after prayer. My husband passed away in his fifties from bone cancer. These were such difficult times. God kept me going. Prayer and good friendships kept me going.

I believe in the power of friendship. Having good connections in life with people is a key to staying strong in the Lord. Keeping on doing things for personal growth, no matter what age you are is also a key that I believe works well. At present I am doing the Keys to

Freedom course. There is no doubt that the enemy is very real. Keeping myself involved and busy within church life and life in general helps me to keep moving forward.

I love meeting new people, helping them feel welcome in our church. I am a trained counsellor in all aspects of counselling. This is very helpful within the ministry that I do at church. I am part of the Welcome team, the Connect team and the Prayer team.

Have I said that friendship is important to me? With that in mind, I co-lead a ministry called Thrive for the over fifty five's. Every two weeks we meet, have lunch, a bit of a laugh and of course a testimony or a word brought by someone. These meetings for some are the only time that some people get out to fellowship and share.

**Jeremiah 29 v 11** *for I know the plans that I have for you, plans to prosper and not harm you.*

I know that God is definitely not finished with me yet.

**Freda Ball age 70+**
Kings Church Bolton
Prayer ministry, Connect ministry and Welcome ministry.
Co-Leading Thrive for the over fifty five's.

# 15

## SEASONS CHANGE

This wonderful woman came into my life through her time with Christians Against Poverty as a befriender. At that point in our life, we had plummeted into over twenty thousand pounds worth of debt. We were homeless living in a friend's basement. Julie showed us such love and understanding through that difficult time and stuck with me as a friend for over thirteen years. Introducing me to a local prayer group of older women where my soul was refreshed weekly for a season.

**Jeremiah 29.11** *"For I know the plans I have for you," declares the LORD, "plans to prosper you and not to harm you, plans to give you hope and a future."*

If you have been blessed in years (as I have) then, like me, you will have experienced many seasons in life. We can look back and see how God's hand has been in our journey, sometimes in ways we would not believe. We all have a story to tell, and our stories can be a great encouragement to others.

May I share one of my seasons?

It was the most painful and saddest time of my life - the loss of my beloved mum. A mum who had always been there for me and my sister. A constant. A wonderful woman.

Mum had experienced many difficulties throughout her life. A broken marriage. A battle with anxiety and agoraphobia. A time when roles were reversed, and my support was needed through a long-troubled period.

Mum reminisced a lot about her times as a teenager, back in the late 1940s, when she and Auntie Rita (her bestie) had hitchhiked 'up hill and down dale', through God's green and pleasant land. So many tales were told of adventures and friends they made along the way. They were great stories to hear, and even more precious now.

Fast-forward many years, with seasons coming and going, and I found myself caring for Mum through the last season of her life when Alzheimer's took residence. Thankfully, she remained the gentle pleasant person we had known, which I am so grateful for.

She took a great liking to the songs of Ken Dodd in this period and his humour would bring her smiles and much laughter, even though she couldn't always follow the script. She enjoyed old hymns too. How music soothes the soul.

But much support was needed as Mum even forgot how to make a cup of tea.

Things moved swiftly over the last weeks but, thankfully, we had a lot of support from our carers, nurses, GP, etc. Mum took to bed, loved and cared for and, within a few weeks, she slipped away from us.

It is so hard to put into words the heartache that followed; the grief, sense of loss and bewilderment, as I tried to move forward without her. She had been a part of my everyday life for sixty-five years.

Weeks and months followed, travelling this painful journey. The first Christmas came, and a new year that Mum wouldn't be in. I was eight months on and definitely not progressing as I thought I should, not fully realising then that there are no hard and fast rules when you are navigating grief.

Then I fell upon something that caught my attention. An outdoor group's walking break in the Peak District. Reading on, it was over in Millers Dale, Derbyshire, staying at the Ravenstor Youth Hostel where Mum and her pal had stayed over seventy years ago! I booked on and talked a friend into going. Perhaps this trip, and retracing Mum's footsteps, could be helpful in my healing journey.

So, a few weeks later, in late February and the coldest season of the year, we found ourselves ready for the great outdoors. We soon got chatting to others, sharing stories. They were delighted to hear that I was there specifically to walk in Mum's footsteps and try to recapture some memories.

All wrapped up on a very chilly February morning, off we went on, what we believed, was a walk for beginners. The scenery was stunning, and the company was good but, four hours in, we seriously considered calling a taxi for our return journey. Well, six hours and twelve miles later, we returned to the hostel, a little worse for wear.

We decided that one day's trekking had been quite enough of the great outdoors adventure. We picked up a lift the next day to Bakewell to take a toot around the village. It was earlyish arriving there. Such a lovely village, well worth a visit. I picked up a homemade Bakewell Tart to take back home.

We heard the church bells chiming up on the hill at the old church, 'calling the faithful'. They certainly drew Debs and me, and we found ourselves, unexpectedly but warmly, welcomed into the Sunday morning fellowship.

God certainly knew where I was at, and the reasons I went on that trip, but I was unaware of just how He was about to minister to those needs in such a special way.

The message shared hit home. It was the story of the ordinary fishermen, Simon and Andrew, whom Jesus called and how they dropped their nets and followed Him.

I recalled a memory from long ago, which is significant in my life and faith journey. May I take you back, over twenty years?

I was a teaching assistant in a local primary school. The journey I had been on to get there was pretty amazing, but not one to share now. After twelve years of working in the school, it was time for something new. Something was stirring. Was it time to move on? I needed God to make it very clear.

The school break came and went and, there I was, having to make a big decision. I can recall on that May morning, when I was due back in school, I was talking to the Lord, imploring him to show me the way. I received a picture in my mind of those fishermen on the shore, seeing Jesus and simply dropping their nets and following His call.

"Why can't I just be like them?" I cried. I had made such a hash of things in the past and had learned from firsthand experience that our ways are not God's ways. He always has the better plan, even though we can't always see it at the time!

Drying my tears, I hurried back to a new term in school. Our deputy head had been meeting with TAs to discuss the following year's classes we would be supporting, and I felt it was only fair to mention that I might be leaving.

A little later, I was out on duty in the playground with dozens of kids milling about, when something caught my eye. Beyond the school fence was a dirt track that led to the car park and just for a moment, one amazing moment, I saw a vision of Jesus. He stretched out his arm and beckoned. He had called them. He called me. Within days, I had put in my resignation and left my wonderful job that summer.

So, there I was, in that church service in Bakewell, being reminded of the calling that God had on my life. It was a distant memory that he clearly reminded me of that morning.

The service continued and some beautiful prayers were shared for needs in the community, for those struggling and those bereaved. Warm caring prayers that ministered to my sad grieving heart like a healing balm.

Towards the end of the service, reflections were shared by a dear elderly lady who, I found out later, was grieving the loss of her husband after a time of caring. But she brought a gentle challenge.

"What part is ours to play?" she asked. "What's next? What is God calling us to?"

There, on that chilly February morning, in an old church in the beautiful Peak District, God ministered in a special way. He reminded me of the calling he has on my life, shared healing.

Prayers and helped me see that it was time for a new season.

Within days of returning home, I knew there had been a change.

The weight had lifted off and I knew that I was now ready to move forward. Had I lingered too long in that painful season, quite possibly, but God still remains in all our seasons and is ready to minister, heal and help us move forward.

"OK Lord,", I said. "You've done it again, you have got your girl back.

What's next Lord? I was back on the up!

It was time for something new. I knew in my heart this wasn't to be in my current church where I had been happily attending for many years.

But I responded to God's nudge, knew where He wanted me to go and am now in a great lively church. I am involved in a new women's ministry. I hope God uses me in this and that I might have the privilege of encouraging other women as they journey through their own seasons of life.

Going back to when I left my job as a teaching assistant you may wonder what happened next?

Well of course God had it all mapped out. No change there then.

You may have heard of the work of CAP (Christians Against Poverty). An amazing debt charity. I had been at a conference a few years previously where an interest was sparked, and a seed was sown. This was the new door I pushed. Our God is so good at opening new doors (and closing them!)

Long story short I spent a few years as a family befriender going on visits with the Debt Coach and then trained to be a debt coach myself and worked in my local community.

I met some great people, and it was such a privilege to journey with families and see them get debt free.

A few years later another season beckoned, and I placed the work down as I journeyed with my dear mum. The hardest season ever.

**Jeremiah 29.11** "For I know the plans I have for you" declares the Lord. "Plans to prosper you and not to harm you. Plans to give you a hope and a future".

**Julie Ricci age 66**

Carmel Community Church Denton.

Serving in women's ministry.

# 16

# YOUNG AT HEART & A HEART FOR THE YOUNG

I first met Pat Harrison and her husband at the mother and toddler group she was running with the team from Pendlebury Church. I had been to a few groups with my little tornado. This was the only one that we stayed at as they really made room for her in the group. My daughter has ADHD amongst other things. Pat also gave me a wonderful opportunity to speak at the Thursday fellowship that she ran for many years at the church.

Pat is the epitome of encouragement, always great to talk to. I'm blessed to be her friend. I loved listening to Pat as she shared her story and loved her enthusiasm for young people.

**Psalm 92 v 14** *"They will still bear fruit in old age; they will stay fresh and green."*

I am a mum to three grown up children. Ruth, Phil and Jonathon. I also have seven grandchildren and I am so very proud of them all, as they all walk with Christ.

I have been married to my husband George for sixty-one years. I made my commitment to follow Jesus when I was seven years of age. As an only child being brought up in a Christian household, I had been to events with my mum and been taught the word from a very early age. I can remember being in a class at Sunday school being told about the importance of asking the Lord into my heart and the knowledge of there being a heaven and a hell. Being aware that as an only child (if I was left behind) I would be all alone, that was not something that I wanted to happen to me. I asked Jesus into my heart in my room that night and have never looked back.

I met my husband George through church. We were married when I was twenty years old. We have served together in the Sunday School classes and over the years many other areas of church ministry, since I was eighteen years old. As we grew together in ministry and in our marriage, we served wherever we could. My husband was an elder and helped organise speakers for services and took care of other needs within the church. I continued in the children's ministry and started a Thursday fellowship where I led and served with my husband for over fifty years. Spending time helping others to grow in their walk with Christ. Teaching others the word of God and praying for people.

In my younger years I worked part time as a nurse while my husband George set up a central heating business which was started in our front room. The business grew and was going very well. We had a business property in Swinton, my husband was very much enjoying the business. One evening out of the blue just as George had come home from work, we got a call to say that the building and all that was in it had gone up in flames. We were devastated but believed at that time that we were to go forward trusting in Him and not in any business. My husband went on to work as a teacher and in management.

In all of my years as a Christian woman I have always loved young people. I ran Christian youth camps for many years enjoying every moment I spent with the young people that came along year after year. I'm blessed even to this day that young men and women still say to me that they remember their time at camp and how God used me and the team to speak to them.

Communicating with others is something that I love doing, whether that is through a phone call, a text or a letter. Encouraging others is something I take very seriously. I feel that it is vital to connect especially with those that are living alone. Sending a message or calling someone who has been missing from church is something that I have always done. If then there was a need for a visit, then that's just what I would do. I love to listen to people and encourage them and pray where I can.

For many years we ran a play group at our church, meeting many of the young Mum's over the years from the local community. Each child that left and started school or nursery was always given a bible, we always played Christian songs for kids at the end of our sessions.

I believe my gifting lies in working with the young people of the church. This possibly stems from running the Sunday school from an early age. I will always encourage the young people no matter how old I get.

I actually believe I am a recycled teenager!

**Pat Harrison age 82**

Kings Church Bolton

Encourager, friend to many and still organises fellowships for older people with George.

# 17

## SELF-CONTROL

**Galatians 5 v 22 - 23** *"But the fruit of the Spirit is love, joy, peace, forbearance, kindness, goodness, faithfulness, 23 gentleness and self-control. Against such things there is no law."*

How many times have I gone completely out of control? Most likely too many times to detail here. As a younger woman I ended up totally out of control on drugs and alcohol. In a complete mess by the time I was twenty-one. Thankfully I accepted Jesus when I was twenty-nine years old and never looked back as the saying goes.

But did I walk in complete control as a Christian woman? As much as it pains me to admit this, the answer is a resounding no, I did not. I became obsessed with reading my bible and attending every meeting that I was physically able to get to. I went to the 6am prayer meeting, went home and got ready to attend the 9am prayer meeting. Stayed at church to clean and glean from the other women that helped out. I helped at the Coffee Morning, attended Bible Studies, Small groups, Prayer meetings and both Sunday services.

To be fair though from where I was coming from none of this excess did me any harm except being a bit on the tired side. It was of course a lack of control needing to be there, needing to please the new people in my life. Wanting to be good at being a Christian! I look back at my Christian walk with open mouthed amazement that I didn't fizzle away or burn out back into my life of drugs and alcohol. I knew without a doubt as the song goes, that "something happened and now I know, He touched me and made me whole". Going back into that darkness was not an option for me.

Growing as a Christian was a very slow process for me. There were some parts of my character that really struggled to die. I got angry so quickly. I remember throwing another Christian man out of my house for saying something that I did not agree with, he desperately wanted me to believe something that was contrary to what my excessive but helpful reading of my bible said. I can't say that I was super polite about it either. Still growing there too. I will never forget being so utterly offended as he left, he was saying that he was wiping the dirt from his shoes on the way out! Thankfully I called my wonderful mentor Nora to tell her about the incident, she calmly explained what he had meant.

Having a mentor and accountability partner was a key point in my growth as a Christian. Nora was someone I was able to tell everything to as she ministered to me through cheese and mayonnaise sandwiches and prayer, I slowly began to 'get it'.

I learned to be more balanced about what I wanted to attend and when. I learned to calm myself when anger bubbled up (often) I carried scriptures around in my pockets to read when I felt angry and a few other negative emotions too.

Rolling into my forties I became a leader. Oh, how important I felt, alongside being terrified of getting it wrong. The scripture better a millstone around your neck than you cause one of my children to stumble, rang through my heart regularly. I was afraid of getting things wrong. Afraid of upsetting or letting my leaders down. I got it wrong often and was rebuked often. Constantly feeling that I was no good at this Christian walk, but knowing without a doubt there was no going back for me.

Along the way God had shown up for me in so many circumstances. Provision financially at exactly the right moment. Provision of a place to stay when we were unceremoniously thrown out of our accommodation at one point. Provision of strong Christian men and women when we were close to the edge of giving up as a couple. All through my years as a Christian God has moved in many different ways. Even miraculously giving me a child when I was fifty.

Moving into my fifties and out of leadership as I began to parent, I started to see where there were still character flaws that needed to be dealt with. I still had this debilitating out of control need to be liked, valued, wanted and loved unconditionally. God was about to bring me into a season of wonderful fullness and healing.

Being forced to look at my own adoption story due to becoming a parent. I was shown in full technicolour glory exactly where my fault lines lay and why they were there. The whole process was utterly devastating and disrupted my whole system. Trust me it needed to be disrupted. It turned out to be the best thing that ever happened to me in my walk with Christ.

He began to show me how much He loved me faults and all, where I had always been told I failed, He showed me every win. Where I had been made to feel so very undervalued and unwanted, He showed me how truly valuable I am and how much I am wanted and loved unconditionally.

It will always be difficult for me to feel loved by people, I may also continue to feel undervalued, but I know that God has healed me in an unimaginable way so that I truly know (not feel) how loved I am. I know my value instead of trying to feel valued.

Practising self-control over my overwhelming feelings is something I continue to work at.

**Fiona Myles 58**

Kings Church Salford

Author of This is me - No darkness too Deep,

This is me - I'm Adopted, Adoption Trauma,

Georgie Me & ADHD, and

The Kings Wonderful Older Women.

All available from my website
www.fionamylesauthor.com or Amazon

# 18

# LOOKING INTO HIS EYES

Lorna is a lovely friend of mine from a shared writing course and our online Team 17 group. Lorna never fails to bring quiet wisdom to any meetings that we have online. Always with a ready smile too. Lorna has written two books so far.

**Luke 13:10-13** *"On a Sabbath Jesus was teaching in one of the synagogues, and a woman was there who had been crippled by a spirit for eighteen years. She was bent over and could not straighten up at all. When Jesus saw her, he called her forward and said to her, 'Woman, you are set free from your infirmity.' Then He put his hands on her, and immediately she straightened up and praised God."*

We know very little about the woman in the passage except that she was bent over and couldn't straighten at all and that she attended a synagogue which would probably have been in someone's home. She would have been in pain and to get to a synagogue would be an effort. I imagine she probably needed some form of stick or sticks to make the journey... or she may even have opened her own home for Sabbath worship. She was a devout woman. Her whole life was ruled by what she could and couldn't do. She couldn't carry anything of any weight as this would pull her over. Even carrying water from the well to her home was impossible. I imagine she often fell when she was moving about, so back pain was not her only physical pain.

She was in emotional pain too. There was that feeling of uselessness and of being a burden, often felt today by older people, who used to be active and helping others, but are now obliged to ask for help for themselves.

But the emotional pain didn't stop there. All she could see was feet and the lower parts of robes. It's difficult to hold a conversation with someone if you can't see their face. Children may have laughed at her or taunted her, adults wondered what sin she had committed to be punished like she was.

At least she could hear what was going on in the synagogue – she could hear Jesus' teaching – even if she couldn't see his face. Can you imagine how it would have felt to be unable to see Jesus's face? To not be able to look into his eyes?

He called her forward and with great effort she moved towards him and looked at his feet.

Initially, I was surprised he didn't go over to her - he must have known the pain she was in. I wonder if it's because he wanted her to get to him, he wanted her to come to him irrespective of the cost.

So she stood there resting on her sticks and looking at his feet. 'You are set free from your infirmity,' but nothing happened until he touched her. Then she stood up and praised God.

Her life had changed, her viewpoint had changed. She could at last, look into Jesus eyes and see the love and joy there. She could see whole people, people she had not seen properly for eighteen years. No wonder she praised God.

Sometimes we have responsibilities pushed onto us or we take on more than we can cope with and they sit heavily on our shoulders, bowing us over. We are crippled with the weight of them and fail to see the joy in the world. Our life has become little more than a series of asks which have to be done and we struggle to cope. Jesus calls us to the foot of the Cross to unload our burdens. He will help us sort through them and dispose of those which could be done by someone else, and then share the weight of those which we have to carry.

But you may say that you don't physically have the time to get to Jesus. What about the odd 'limbo' minutes – the times you are waiting for the kettle to boil, when you're washing up or loading and unloading the dishwasher, when you're doing housework, driving or waiting in a queue at the supermarket? All these times and many other limbo times can be used to talk to Jesus. We all have time for a little prayer each day and that is all he asks of us, to come to Him.

And for those whose lives feel non-productive, even if we are bedbound, we can pray for others, phone someone else to see how they are and listen to them and pray.

Jesus wants everyone to come to him, to see his face and to look into his eyes.

## Lorna Clark age 72

Licensed Lay Minister (CofE) in the parishes of Lingwood, Strumpshaw, South Burlingham and Hassingham, attending all four-rota dependent.

Lorna's books - Strawberries and Suspicions and Breadcrumbs and Bones (genre cosy crime) both available from Amazon.

# 19

# COURAGE AND ENCOURAGE

I met Joanna through my husband, Joanna is a valued volunteer at the Community Grocery Bolton. I knew that she had gone through a difficult time recently and hoped that she would be happy to share a piece for this book. A wise woman indeed.

**Joshua 1 v 9** *"Have I not commanded you? Be strong and courageous. Do not be afraid; do not be discouraged, for the Lord your God will be with you wherever you go."*

I have led a very happy, blessed life so far, then last year, at the age of 62, I received the diagnosis of breast cancer! As you can imagine it was quite a shock, but I was told early on in the journey that the prognosis was good. I had surgery to remove the cancer and 3 weeks of radiotherapy and tests showed that the cancer hadn't spread and that I did not need chemotherapy which was a great relief. During the initial phase of treatment my faith was challenged more than it ever had been, but with the support and prayers of my husband, family, Church family and Christian friends I really felt my faith grow more than any other time in my life and grew closer and closer to God. He felt so real, so close and so precious.

During these tough weeks I received many messages, cards and texts with Bible verses and even a 'meal deal'! which really helped and encouraged us. I could not believe how many people cared enough about me so much. The many verses gave us much encouragement that God had not finished with me yet and I would have a future.

**Jeremiah 29 v 11** was a favourite of my mum's and really resonated with me too during this time.

**Jeremiah 29 v 11** *'For I know the plans I have for you, declares the Lord, plans to prosper you and not to harm you, plans to give you a hope and a future.'*

**Psalm 23** kept popping into my mind, maybe as I knew it by heart. It is not particularly a favourite Psalm, but its words really lifted and supported me. I'm sure many of you could recite it or the words to the several hymns and worship songs based on its words. Also, our grand-daughter gave me a picture she had drawn when I was admitted to hospital, depicting the words from **Psalm 23 v 4**, which was a great comfort.

*"Even though I walk through the darkest valley, I will fear no evil, for you are with me; your rod and your staff, they comfort me."*

A while after my treatment had finished our pastor asked me to bring the devotion at our early morning prayer meeting, I had lost confidence during this time but felt God speaking to me about this Psalm and the idea of verse 4 and the rod and staff kept coming to mind.

During all this experience I felt no fear, even lying on a trolley waiting for surgery I felt like I was wrapped in a thick duvet, protecting and comforting me. I know this was due to the pastoral team and prayer group at Church, my family and all my Christian friends holding me in prayer, they were my rod and staff. I really felt God telling me this. In this Psalm the rod is a symbol of The Lord's strength and protection and the staff of guidance and reassurance. Never forget how the support you can offer and especially prayers are essential for people going through tough times. This really helps and comforts them in their faith journey through it all. Praying for each other is so important, especially times when we can't pray for ourselves.

I have kept all the cards I was sent I have kept them all in a scrapbook with all the verses written around them to remind me of the love, care and encouragement I was shown, I will never forget this and pray that God will continue to use me to encourage other people and to lift people in need to God.

1. Can you try to memorise scripture more often as it may help in times of need when the Holy Spirit prompts us with these words either for yourself or to share with a friend.

2. Read **Psalm 23** prayerfully asking God to speak to you through it.

3. Ask God to lead you to someone you could encourage today with a word of scripture, prayer or a message.

**2 Cor 1 v 3-4** *"Praise be to the God and Father of our Lord Jesus Christ, the Father of compassion and the God of all comfort, who comforts us in all our troubles, so that we can comfort those in any trouble with the comfort we ourselves receive from God."*

**Joanna Connor age 62**
Kings church Bolton
Volunteer at the Community Grocery Bolton

# 20

## ALL THINGS ARE POSSIBLE

Debbie is from the wonderful U.S.A. I had noticed that she had written her own story about her life containing some awful seasons of abuse which she has turned into a survivor's guide. She writes with such openness and honesty. I was over the moon when she agreed to share a small portion of her story with us.

**Mark 9 v 23** *"Jesus said to him, if you can believe, all things are possible to him who believes."*

There have been times in my life when I have wondered why God has allowed bad things to happen to me, or my family members. The older I have grown, and the closer I've gotten to God, the more I realise that everything that has happened was sifted through God's hands and that He must allow me to suffer consequences of my poor decisions.

During the Covid crisis I lost my major stream of income for nine months. So did my adult son, who was responsible for major expenses for his ex-wife and children. I realised in June of 2020 that my reserve funds were going to run out by the end of the year and if I wanted to protect my financial future and be able to retire someday, I would need to sell my home of seventeen and a half years. I had inherited my home from my parents, as I needed to move to something smaller. To further complicate things, I was separated from my third husband of five years, who was a malignant narcissist, and he would not leave until the house was sold.

I was at total peace with selling my home even though I had no idea where God was moving me or when. My ex and I had agreed at some point that we could file our own divorce paperwork and save the expense of attorneys, but he wanted some of the equity from my home. I did ask him if he had prayed about that, since he claimed to be a Christian and he had not contributed to any of the loan payments or improvements. He became angry and started yelling that he did not have to ask God because the law told him he could and stormed out of the room, slamming the door behind him.

Fortunately, my Christian friends and my close walk with Jesus during this time kept me calm and at peace. I hoped we would divorce quickly, and I would be able to use my equity to purchase a new home right away. That however was not to be the case.

The house sold ten days after going on to the market and before I could return from my son's to pack up my remaining belongings. My ex-husband had filed for divorce without my knowledge and had paperwork drawn up by an attorney saying he would get half of the equity and none of the debt and planned to have me served at the closing of the sale. My only choice would have been to accept his terms or lose the sale.

I figured out just in time how to stop that scenario from happening, but the result was having all the equity tied up for another six months; this meant that I had to find a room to rent. A wonderful sister in Christ who had once been in a similar situation was willing to rent me a beautiful and comfortable room quite reasonably until I would be able to get a new home of my own. I ended up being there for 14 months!

God kept me in the palm of His hand and gave me perfect peace during what I call my "wilderness experience." At sixty seven years old, for the first time in my adult life, I did not own my own home. I prayed every day and thanked God in advance for the home he had already picked out for me. My work returned and I was able to restore my credit, pay down my debt, and eventually purchase a much smaller home closer to the beach; my happy place. My Christian friends have been supporting me and praying for me every step of the way. God placed me in a tiny neighbourhood in a tiny town with much less traffic than Orlando where I previously lived. My neighbours are wonderful, caring, and helpful. I found a new church that preaches the truth from scripture and have made some new friends close to my age.

God allowed me to suffer the consequences I brought on myself for marrying a man that I knew was not the love of my life, but pressured me into believing we were meant for each other and would have a "Hallmark" ending to our lives. I felt the Holy Spirit warn me, but I married him anyway. God held me close through it all, and gave me the gift of a new life in a new home in a new neighbourhood with some new wonderful friends. He ALWAYS knows what is best for me when I cannot see it myself. I give Him all the praise and glory and honour for all the good He has done in my life as He has been healing my hurts.

**James 1 v 17** *"Every good and perfect gift is from above, coming down from the Father of heavenly lights, who does not change like shifting shadows."*

**Debbie Bias, age 70**
Cross Bridge Church in Rockledge, FL
Love, Betrayal, Rebound: A Survivor's Guide
www.lighthousebutterfly.com

# 21

## OVERCOMING BY FAITH AND THE WORD OF TESTIMONY

What can I say about Ann? Most importantly without Ann and her extraordinary faith and prayers you would most likely not be reading this book. I was so happy when she agreed to write a piece for me. God has used this woman in a mighty way in countless lives. Including mine.

**Revelation 12 v 11** *"And they overcame him by the blood of the Lamb, and by the word of their testimony; and they loved not their lives unto death."*

You know the expression, 'You couldn't write it?'

Well, I'm writing it.

In my forties I had boundless energy. I was a Glasgow street pastor and I loved it. I would work until nine at night, caring for people with physical and learning disabilities. I would then go into Glasgow until four in the morning, ministering on the streets. I prayed for healing and saw people come to know the Lord. We even helped save a few lives. I was also a director of Healing Rooms in Bo'ness. We saw people come out of the occult and get saved. I had favour at work and was asked to become acting manager and to go and help start a new service away from home.

Suddenly, I was in the deep end out of my depth. The new service was very challenging. One night, I returned badly scratched and bleeding on my neck. I was suddenly feeling vulnerable and deflated.

It was after midnight when I entered the hotel, and I was exhausted. It turned out the receptionist was a witch and she started opening up to me. Her spells were all backfiring on her and she wanted out but was scared. I was able to minister to her and gave her the book 'From Witchcraft to Christ.' God sent another spirit-filled Christian to work with me and we prayer-covered each other. Things changed radically and the peace and love of God came into the service. The person who had scratched me badly became like a gentle lamb and we learned to communicate without words. It was such a blessed time.

Just before my 50th birthday I learned to drive and was so blessed to get a new car. The world was my oyster. Then bang: a van smashed into my car and my neck, back and leg were badly injured. I was attending a chiropractor for months.

I then went to a Christian Conference in Glasgow. The speaker said there is someone sitting to my right who was injured in a car accident and God wants to heal you. I suddenly felt this power go up and down my spine. I began to move about, unrestricted, and was dancing about. A few days later I went to my chiropodist, and he confirmed my healing. Praise God.

Would you believe it, another accident? I banged the back of my head off a metal pole in a bus accident. I ended up with post-concussion syndrome. My mobility, coordination and eyesight were affected. I went to an optician, and he photographed me behind my eye.

Now this is where the scripture all things work to the good comes in. The photographs revealed that I had narrow angle glaucoma and could have suddenly gone blind or have permanent vision loss. Praise God, mine was detected.

I was sent to the hospital. I remember saying to the optometrist, "You can't put drops in my eyes as I have narrow angle glaucoma and I could have a closed angle attack and go blind."

He said to me that my retina might be detaching, and I could go blind. Thankfully it turned out my retina wasn't detaching, and God has also healed my eyesight. The closing angles in my eyes have now opened and I am no longer at risk of going blind.

So, I came through all of that, and then along came Covid. I have asthma and it affected me badly. I actually thought at one point this could be my time to go home. I had peace and absolutely no fear. I felt the tangible presence of God so close. One particular night I couldn't get breath in my lungs. I was physically exhausted; I couldn't even fight back anymore. All I thought was, "Jesus carry me."

Then ping. My phone lit up with a message from my friend Sandra. It said to cover myself in the blood. As I prayed, I felt a wind blowing on my face and air go into my lungs. Now the miracle of this answer to prayer was that Sandra sent this text on Friday, but I didn't receive it until Saturday night, at the exact moment I needed it. God's perfect timing.

The incredible thing was my oxygen levels actually rose to higher than before I had Covid. I just love how God restores us to better than we were before.

Then the news came that my mum had stage four ovarian cancer. I remember sitting in the hospital and I said to the Lord, "I love you and I praise you." No matter what news you hear, don't let the enemy steal your love and praise of

God. That praise was to sustain me over the next two years.

Worship, laughter and joy will strengthen you.

As you get older you often find yourself with more caring responsibilities and that is when you need God's strength and to praise. "The joy of the Lord is our strength." Nehemiah 8.10. When my mum, husband and I all got Covid on the same day, we had a praise party and found things to thank God for. We had such a laugh and, praise God, my mum came through it fine, even with cancer.

In addition to caring for my mum and working I also took care of my sister with severe bipolar disorder and looked after three houses.

I was in my sister's garden praying and pulling out huge weeds. I was physically exhausted. My sister was in hospital after a psychotic episode. I prayed for the Lord to send us help. Then I turned around. Each place I pulled out a large weed a small white feather appeared. I knew God had heard my prayer.

Every time my friend, Anne Brown, prayed for me she kept getting the words 'pray for strength.'

It's so important to have prayer cover and find faithful friends. A lot of friends stop visiting and calling when you are caring for someone with cancer. I guess they just don't know what to say. It's like you're in a bubble with your loved one and God. Time moves so slowly, but it is precious time.

My dear friend Christine Matthews also helped me to stay on fire for Jesus during the hardest season of my life. She truly has been a faithful friend. She's in her early 70s and a mighty woman of God. She literally is a walking miracle. She should have been dead from a bad operation. Her surgeon called her his miracle patient. She can preach and see a dead church come on fire with repentance and full surrender to God. Christine has actually seen her own husband Derek raised from the dead. Christine's husband had a heart attack in the park opposite them, where there has been a lot of witchcraft. Derek fell twice. The paramedic checking Derek at the hospital said to Christine that she wasn't telling him everything. He knew Derek had been dead from the heart readings. Christine confirmed he had been dead. Praise Jesus for his resurrection life.

Christine and I read this book about Ma Jenkins. She didn't start her ministry until her 60s. She had been blind, and God healed her. God would tell her to go places. She just listened and obeyed. She would just go, and God would provide the transport. She would turn up and pray and miracles took place. One story was she walked into a hospital and prayed; Siamese twins get separated.

It's so simple. Wait on God. Hear his voice and instructions and obey. Pray in simple faith and watch God do the miracles. All the glory is His alone.

My mum, Elizabeth Borland, was a woman of faith and took her strength from God. She overcame so many odds. I nicknamed her Tigger because she kept bouncing back. The cancer nurse Mel couldn't explain how she was still on her feet. She was a walking miracle.

Once, the doctor told us to prepare ourselves that she would be gone that weekend. Come Monday morning she was up smiling making a fried breakfast.

She was in hospital, and they overdosed her on antibiotics, her kidneys could have been damaged.

Then we got told the two tumours on her ovaries were massive and she didn't have long to live. Also, she had a fistula tear, and they were considering operating and putting in a stoma bag.

She turned to me and said that she was worried about a woman opposite her in the ward that she was losing her faith. She asked me to go and pray for her. I did and I prayed for others too.

The people in that ward had been so depressed and had given up until my mum appeared. She brought laughter, life and hope. The atmosphere in the place totally shifted.

The nurse told me that my mum could be in hospital for months as there were no care packages. I prayed and said, "Lord, you need to get her out of here." That afternoon I got a call to say she was getting home that night. She was sprung and the next week we were off on holiday together.

During the night when my mum was dying, Jesus said to me to get out of bed and dance. I was exhausted but I climbed out of bed and began to dance. I felt him embrace me in his love. It was that love that was to sustain me and give me strength to look after my mum on her final day.

Less than an hour before the nurses came back with a syringe driver, my mum passed into glory. I kissed her on the head, and I said we loved her, and God loved her. I played "How great though art" and she was gone. My husband said at that exact moment the bedroom filled with light.

The greatest privilege we have is to sit with our loved ones and see them go into the presence of Jesus. I'm not saying it will be easy. We are human and our hearts will break but He heals the broken hearted and comforts us as only

He can. As we wait on Him and feel His love and presence we will laugh again and renew our strength.

As we get older, we realise all our strength comes from Him. We can do nothing without Him. We also learn that every test becomes a testimony. "They overcame him by the blood of the lamb and by the Word of their testimony" Revelations 12.11. Never stop praising Jesus' name and testifying of His goodness and glory.

## Ann Mackie age 58

Ann is learning under Prayer rival ministries; she has been a street pastor and was on the core team for Pray for Scotland for ten years. A Healing Rooms director in Bo'ness for a season and has spoken and given testimony in many churches over the years. Also praying in many countries across the world.

# 22

# I LOVE JESUS

Helen as a valued volunteer works with my husband in the Community Grocery within Kings Church Bolton. Always on hand to help out with picking up donations for the shop, which helps out the local community in times of need. I had a great afternoon listening to Helen's story and was blown away by her inner strength and love for Jesus.

**Hebrews 10 v 35** *"Therefore, do not cast away your confidence, which has great reward."*

I was not brought up in a church environment. Maybe just the usual Sunday service at Easter or an occasion. My grandparents though were from the Methodist church where my Grandad was a preacher. I would imagine that prayer would have been sent my way.

I left home at an early age to get married. My parents were quite strict and did not like the young man that I was going out with. I was earning my own money so decided that it was time to move out as the tensions at home were rising. I married at a fairly young age thinking it was going to be a great love story. Unfortunately for me the marriage became a very difficult place for me to be. My husband was manipulative and controlling. Not allowing me to be myself or have any time for myself. I stayed in that marriage for nineteen long hard years, feeling weaker and weaker as the years went on. Anxiety and stress became my best friends. I eventually got out of that marriage.

I remarried thinking things would be different, but I found myself facing the same kind of controlling behaviour. This marriage ended after I had an affair with someone else. Again, I found myself in a place where anxiety and stress were huge in my life. I also began to feel depressed and at times wondering what was the point of being here.

Throughout these turbulent years I remained friends with Andy and Elaine, a strong Christian couple who regularly told me they were praying for me and often invited me to church. I can remember having a job once where I passed a church on a daily basis and often thought about going in, but I never did. Finding myself single again, a friend of mine was looking for somewhere to stay temporarily, so I invited her to come and stay with me in Heald Green. She was also single and introduced me to Tinder, the dating app. I joined just for the amusement factor and within half an hour I had a date with a guy called Chris. I didn't know it then, but I was off to dinner with my husband to be from what I thought was just a bit of fun with my friend. Never underestimate the moves God is making in your life.

Chris was a Christian and we hit it off straight away. We had a lovely time. Chris and I lived together for two years before we got married. We have been blissfully married for six years now. Chris had a church of his own where he went to worship, but we needed something that truly suited us both. We found Kings Church Bolton where I fully and truly accepted the Lord Jesus Christ as my saviour. I was baptised at Kings Church Bolton on November the twentieth 2022.

I absolutely love making connections with people. I serve in the Blend Cafe at church, I volunteer in the Community Grocery, I serve in the toddlers' group and I enjoy serving in the community groups meeting new Christians and non-Christians.

We have three dogs, one of which is a Basset Hound puppy. In the future I would love to Foster. There is no limit to the amount of love that I have to give, so my age should not be anything that holds me back either.

So, what's changed since I gave my life to Christ? I would say that before Jesus came into my life I had a lot of stress, anxiety and a level of depression. I felt empty most of the time. I'm positive that my main issue was not forgiving others. I was carrying a ton of baggage from how I had been treated by my previous partners, my family and friends, the people that you would think should care the most about you. Not all of them, but enough to cause harm and resentment inside of me. Learning to forgive has relieved me of a huge burden. I firmly believe I would not have been able to do that without the teachings of Jesus. Also realising that forgiving these people didn't necessarily mean that I had to let them back into my life to hurt me again, but that I could still move on and not allow myself to go back there but to simply let it go.

It also occurred to me that none of those people were Christians. My Christian friends have stood by me through everything and even in my darkest hours have never once criticised or judged me, simply they have continually prayed for me through it all.

**Joshua 1 v 9** *"Have I not commanded you? Be strong and courageous. Do not be afraid; do not be discouraged, for the LORD your God will be with you wherever you go."*

**Matthew 5 v 44** *"But I tell you, love your enemies and pray for those who persecute you."*

These are two scriptures that among many more mean a lot to me, that I refer to when I need to. Do you have verses that you can refer to when times are feeling tough? If not, find one or two and keep them in your pocket or tape them to your fridge door.

I never fail to be moved by just how blessed I am.

**Helen Allen age 61**

Kings Church Bolton

Volunteer at the Community Grocery Bolton

Blend cafe volunteer and

Self-employed bookkeeper

# 23

# HERE I AM, STILL STANDING

Thank you, Heather, for agreeing to write a piece for the book. Thank you for all that you have done to help me to feel welcome in church. Heather co leads the Thrive group for over fifty fives. A truly godly woman, filled with the Holy Spirit.

**Psalm 92 14-15** tells us that *"we shall still bear fruit in old age… proclaiming "The Lord is upright He is my rock…."*

When I was young there were no mobile phones, Netflix, X boxes, even home telephones were rare. Children used to play jacks and hopscotch, the girls played two balls against the wall or even three and four balls if you were good enough.

Being brought up in a Christian family, church was the centre of most things in our home with youth groups and other activities at church. We often had visiting missionaries telling us tales of what it was like in Africa. I found it fascinating. Some of us had an autograph book and we would ask them to write something in it and sign it, one even painted a little picture for me of an African village, with mud huts and palm trees.

At some point I must have asked my dad to make an entry. He wrote "I know Him by experience I've proved Him many a day and what experience has taught me; no man can take away" Alongside it in childish handwriting I had written "I love you Jesus". I was about seven years of age.

Childhood was a safe place for me, and I firmly believed that my dad and God could fix anything but then I was only a child and had little experience of many things.

That was many years ago now. I have walked my own pathway with God since. It has brought many experiences of my own, some of them wonderful, others more difficult. But then this is life and through it all we are assured that God is faithful, His promises over our lives are yes and amen in Jesus. Life brings many challenges-to our health-to our faith and unless our foundation is secure and firm we will flounder. I have had to learn to stand upon the rock Christ Jesus. When the waters are swirling around us and we are struggling, then as our feet are firmly planted we are safe because He is immovable in His faithfulness.

How do we get to that place of knowing we are safe, you may ask, how do we stand firm when circumstances are uncertain and we feel anything but safe? This is what I have learnt. Read the promises of God in His word; speak them out in faith as you navigate the uncertainty. Share with trusted friends who can stand with you. Ecclesiastes 4:12 says *a cord of three strands is not easily broken* so the Holy Spirit as the third strand brings strength and guidance and above all share it with your Heavenly Father, as it says in Philippians 4:6-7 *Be anxious for nothing, but in everything by prayer and supplication with Thanksgiving let your requests be known to God….. And you will have peace.*

There have been many times when even my faith has been shaky, but He has never failed me and coming out the other side I can see that His hand has been in all things. He is Faithful.

We used to sing a song, *Through it all, through it all,* I've learnt to trust in Jesus I've learnt to trust in God. Through it all I've learnt to depend upon His word. (Have a listen to it Andréa Crouch wrote it)

**Psalm 92 14-15** tells us that *"we shall still bear fruit in old age… proclaiming "The Lord is upright He is my rock…. "*

So, I ask you what is on your heart, what area is of concern to you then ask the Lord to show you how to bear fruit in that area.

And so here I am still standing because of Jesus. Many things have changed as the years have gone by, but one thing still remains the same as I write "I love you Jesus". (In slightly better handwriting than before.

## Heather Denney age 72

Payroll manager for many years.

Kings Church Bolton

Heather co leads Thrive for over fifty fives, part of the prayer team and volunteers on reception at church. She is currently facilitating the Keys to Freedom Course.

And of course, does Grandma duties as and when needed.

# 24

# COME UNTO ME

I was so blessed reading Ann's piece for this book. Menopause is so underestimated in the difficulties that it can cause. The battle is real, but here Ann has shared some wonderful scriptures that have carried her through the tough times. Her candid account of what she has gone through, I hope that it will help others that are suffering in a similar way. We are all unique and Menopause is not a one size fits all thing.

**Matthew 11 v 28** *"Come unto me all ye that labour and are heavy Laden and I will give you rest."*

I have been on the menopause now for twenty-five years. It started when I was thirty-eight years old. I am now sixty-three. I have heard some ladies say that they have breezed through with no symptoms and I have heard some say, give it a couple of years and you will be "out the other side", but for some ladies like me, the menopause can last for years and years with no sign of being out the other side.

Twenty-five years ago, nobody talked much about menopause, so when I was offered the chance to take hormone replacement therapy, commonly referred to as

HRT, I took it. Everything was fine for a few years until suddenly I was told, sorry but that is it, you have been on HRT long enough. When the doctor tells you to finish, you stop straight away.

Shortly after I had finished the HRT treatment, I was invited to have my first mammogram at a breast screening clinic at my local hospital. The screening showed that there was a lump in my breast. I was told it was probably caused by me being on HRT. After a two week wait which felt like two years, I was told the lump was a cyst, the relief was wonderful, but it had plunged me into a dark place. I should have taken all my fears to the lord but instead I tried to cope with it all on my own.

**Isaiah 41 v 13** *"For I the lord thy God will hold thy right hand, saying unto thee, fear not. I will help thee."*

so now I carried on with no medication trying to get through with all the many symptoms that come with stopping that came my way, when I found another lump, this time it was in a different place and in a more intimate area back again to the hospital where I was given another two week wait which felt like another two years again I was told that it was another cyst and again the relief was immense but I had not learned from the last time I was in the same situation.

Joshua 1v9 *Have I not commanded d be strong and good courage be not afraid neither be Thou dismayed for the Lord thy God is with thee whithersoever thou goest.*

What I did not realise at the time was beside all the physical symptoms came the mental symptoms as well. As I had been left in a very dark mood after all the hospital visits, I was prescribed antidepressants, they did help a little, but it was not enough to help me deal with all the symptoms I was suffering from. Out of all the thirty or so symptoms that are associated with the menopause I ticked almost all of the boxes. Ranging from hot sweats, insomnia, depression, hair loss, dental problems, itchy skin, brain fog, anxiety attacks and more. Each one as debilitating as the next. The list seemed endless. When would I "be out the other side"

**1st Chronicles 16 v 11** *"Seek the lord and his strength, seek his face continually."*

There was a period in my life where I was having so many palpitations that I thought I was having a heart attack. At other times when I was forgetting so much, I thought I was in the early stages of dementia and let's not forget all the many trips to the dentist when I was told that all the problems I was experiencing were because I hadn't been cleaning my teeth properly. I knew that was not right because I have always cleaned my teeth properly, flossing every day. All of these problems were brought on with the menopause.

**Psalm 73 v 26** *"My Flesh and my heart fails but God is the strength of my heart and my portion forever."*

Despite all that I have experienced in the years since I started on this "Journey" I do feel that I am in the best time of my life. I have a loving and supportive family, I belong to a wonderful church family and more importantly I belong to an amazing God who loves me and cares for me.

**Proverbs 31:25** *"Strength and honour are her clothing, and she shall rejoice in time to come."*

**Ann Tetterington age 63**

Blend cafe

Mum and Grandma

'Who let the dads out' bacon butty maker.

# 25

# THE JOY OF FORGIVENESS

My dear friend Marcia has two pieces in this book. A wonderful and incredible woman who has given me the privilege of being her friend for over twenty years. Sticking by me through good times and not so good times. At one time being solely responsible for keeping a roof over our heads. As Marcia has walked through her own good and not so good times. I have watched her walk with a magnificent grace and sensitivity to the Holy Spirit.

**Psalm 32 v 1-2** *"Blessed is he whose transgression is forgiven, whose sin is covered. Blessed is the man to whom the LORD does not impute iniquity, and in whose spirit there is no deceit."*

For many years, I was what many would probably call a "Good Christian". I attended services regularly, paid tithes, was active in serving my church family, loved Jesus (of course) and was active in sharing the Gospel with those who didn't know Him.

Then disaster struck. Not suddenly, or out of the blue. Instead, it crept up on me gradually with my lowering, and then total abandonment of biblical standards. Along with this came the shifting of my focus and changes in my motivation. No longer were my actions totally "Christ-centred". Stretched in my responsibilities for my family, work and church, I decided I deserved some personal happiness too.

With my eyes tightly closed and ignoring the Spirit's voice until it quietened to a mere whisper, I danced with the devil uncomfortably for some time. I justified every step on the basis that I was not doing anything wrong, and I was not really hurting anyone, quite the opposite.

Beware, Satan is truly a great liar, and can deceive us regardless of our age.

Eventually, the disco ball fell, the dance floor collapsed, and my life was left shattered and ruined along with it.

Dejected, churchless and feeling friendless, lonely and lost, I sought the help of the One I had been continuing to preach to others about, whilst not disciplining myself, as advised by Paul in Corinthians.

**1 Cor 9.27** *"But I discipline my body and bring it into subjection, lest, when I have preached to others, I myself should become disqualified."*

I was on the verge of disqualification but took the Lord at His word to make things right, if I just confessed my sins.

**1 John 1 v 9** *"If we confess our sins, He is faithful and just to forgive us our sins and to cleanse us from all unrighteousness."*

It was not an easy task facing up to my failings. What a huge and disgusting pile of garbage I had to own up to creating. I still ask myself sometimes, "Where was Marcia when this rotting pile was building up? Couldn't she smell it?

Sin has consequences, and though I know I was instantly forgiven by God when I confessed, I had to humble myself and offer painful personal apologies to a number of people affected by my behaviour. After the confession, came the joy and freedom of forgiveness, as Jesus proved Himself to be just and faithful indeed. Oh, what a sweet sensation that will never ever leave me.

I still occasionally offer apologies to people I have not seen for many years. No longer a painful process though, this now serves to re-ignite my joy, when I consider the restoration and abundant blessings lavished on me by my Father since those dark days.

Amongst the blessings I count the faithful friends who have heeded Paul's further advice in

**2 Cor 2. 5-8** *"But if anyone has caused grief.......you ought rather to forgive and comfort him, lest perhaps such a one be swallowed up with too much sorrow. Therefore I urge you to reaffirm your love to him."*

Rather than remaining desperately unhappy, and useless, the forgiveness, comfort and love I have received have spurred me on to accept the many opportunities the Lord has given me to share about his deep love and care for those who feel ashamed, guilty and far from Him, just as I had.

The doors that have swung open for me have been amazing! God has been so gracious. I think the Samaritan woman who Jesus met at the well in John 4 may have been an older lady, given that she had had the opportunity to be involved in six serious relationships, by the time Jesus met her.

Just like this great, early evangelist, who was able to draw many other Samaritans to believe in Jesus, despite her questionable past, God has put me in places where I can experience the thrill of seeing others come to know Him too. I could say, despite my history, but maybe it is because of my history, given that those who are forgiven much, love much.

**Marcia Shields**

Family Solicitor

Age 65

Shoreline Calvary Chapel North London

Worked with various Christian drug rehabilitation services. Prison chaplaincy volunteer for many years.

# 26

# IN GOD'S STRENGTH

I kept Sandy's piece till the end because she has written in such a happy, friendly, conversational style. With her God bless you all at the end, I felt it was a fitting end to the 'Wonderful Older Women' part. I see Sandy helping out everywhere. Always with a big smile on her face. Looking fabulous at the same time. Thank you so much for agreeing to write this piece.

**John 3 v 16** *"For God so loved the world that he gave his one and only Son, that whoever believes in him shall not perish but have eternal life."*

Hi, my name is Sandy Hampson. I have just turned 66 years of age and what a celebration that feels for me. "Really I hear you say" I will tell you why!

I'm happily married and have been for forty-five years. we met in a nightclub (which is funny because that's the last place you would find me now) That must have been 1975. We have two lovely children, a son & daughter. They have two children each which means we have four absolutely gorgeous grandchildren, three boys and one girl, ranging from fourteen to four in age. All healthy and doing well.

We feel very blessed.

I am one of six children, brought up in a loving household but also quite chaotic as you can imagine, we didn't have much but somehow rubbed along together and got on with things. Being the oldest I was always busy doing stuff, sorting things out, sorting my siblings out, helping around the house, babysitting etc. I remember going to Sunday school as a child but don't remember anything about what we were taught in it. I obviously remember going to school but don't remember being pushed or encouraged to do well, hence I don't think I left school with much in the way of certificates or exams passed.

As you will have established, I was married young and had my children young. I was always a key member in their schools with many roles, spinning plates constantly as a young mum. I worked job's part-time until my children went to senior school. As the children were older, I applied to go to university and qualified as a social worker. I loved my job, it was right up my street, problem solving, helping people and being paid for it too!

My mum was a real godly woman, she went to church, and I remember "songs of praise" were always on the television on Sunday evenings.

I never understood the connection and what she got out of it. Later in life she would invite me to things at her church and I would always decline saying I'm too busy or NO it's not for me but you enjoy it (quite patronising when I think back)

If only I knew then what I know now! Which is: God is my saviour. For God so loved the world that he gave his one and only son that whoever believes in him shall not perish but have eternal life. (John 3.16.)

I've had many hiccups along the way in my life as a child, as a teenager and certainly as an adult. One of the life changing events was when my son made some bad decisions in his life. Another was when I lost my mum. Another when one of my sisters was extremely ill.

There are more but not enough page space to share here, but my point is: we all have issues, troubles and life changing events.

It was during… let's call it my first storm. I felt desperate, I didn't know what else to do to support my son. Keep in mind I'm good at this sort of thing. I've done it all my life. But let me tell you when it's so close to home it's difficult. Your heart rules your head big time.

I started to go to church with my mum, I found it amazing, loved the preach, loved the worship but wasn't sure on how I was feeling. I could not stop crying, my husband used to say, "what are you going there for? It does nothing but upset you". I of course now know it was the Holy Spirit working within me, helping me, supporting me, sorting me out (like I'd done for others). I very quickly did many courses, Alpha being the first one. I learnt so much more about God and found that this was the only way forward, to put my trust in Him. I was baptised and became a Christian. This was back in 2009. (why did I decline all those invitations from my mum) I don't know, but GOD does. His timing is perfect. I truly understand the connection now and its WOW.

I attend Kings Church in Bolton where I have a lovely church family. I am now a very involved active member of church life, again supporting and helping others. I am also a hands-on Grandma, A Loving and helpful sister (two of which have been saved), aunty and friend to many and of course a good mother and wife. (well, I think my hubby would agree).

I have learnt to give things to GOD and He will help where it is needed. I have learnt to pray and to listen to GODs voice. I have learnt to read His word and from all of this I feel his peace and you will too.

What I would say to younger women reading this, is, you are a child of GOD (John 1.12) be on fire for GOD don't spin those plates alone, be helped and supported. You are fearfully and wonderfully made (psalm 139.14)

I couldn't do what I do in my own strength, and neither can you and more to the point, you really don't have to. I often wish I'd have realised this sooner in life.

Remember I said I was celebrating being sixty-six years of age! well through all the trials and tribulations of childhood, adolescence, adulthood I've now made it to state pension age. With God's help. I'm now a senior with a free bus pass and a train pass. So happy birthday to me and happy travelling around. What more could you want with Jesus at the centre.

God Bless you all.

**Sandy Hampson age 66**
Kings Church Bolton
Friend to many

Allow me to introduce you to my friend Georgia in Chapter 26. She may not be a Wonderful Older Woman, but she is an inspiration to many.

# 27

# GEORGIA FORSYTH - BARNABAS THE ENCOURAGER

**Acts 11:23** *"When Barnabas arrived and saw what God had been kind enough to do for them, he was very glad. So, he begged them to remain faithful to God with all their hearts."*

My lovely friend Georgia asked me if she could have a part in this book. Although she is nowhere near the fifty-five-year-old minimum age to be in the book, I just could not say no.

Georgia is thirty-five years old and lives independently in Key housing in a small town in Scotland. Georgia sent me the following words that she wanted in the book to help show that even with Down's syndrome she is a wonderful woman of God.

I have been a devoted follower of God, He has been my rock, and He has shown me that in His mighty presence, everything is possible in His name. While I was born with down's syndrome and I want to say for families out there with children with disabilities, just remember you can be who you are and don't let anyone tell you what you should do. Belief in God has given me a chance to show in me that He is working in my life.

I have known Georgia since she was a little girl. Watching her grow and become a wonderful young woman has been a joy. I was recently at a women's event at Georgias church, we shared the same table. Being able to watch my friend worship God was a delight. Her smile lights up any room. Having the heart of an encourager Georgia always makes me feel ten feet tall.

Thank you, Georgia, for your contribution to the book, and for all the encouragement over the years.

# ACKNOWLEDGEMENTS

To God goes all the glory for this book.

To all the amazing women who gave of their time, their hearts and their wisdom and experience. I thank you all from the bottom of my heart. I have had the desire to do a book of this type for many years. It is the kind of book that I personally like to read. Testimony and the word of God never fail to lift my spirit.

*Ann Hallows*

*Ann Tetterington*

*Marcia Shields*

*Nora Hutcheson*

*Heather Denney*

*Sandy Hampson*

*Pat Harrison*

*Lorna Clarke*

*Julie Ricci*

*Lisa Dickinson*

*Joanna Connor*

*Vanessa Holmes*

*Ann Mackie*

*Iris Hennessy*

*Tina Voordouw*

*Heather Cunningham*

*Freda Ball*

*Georgia Forsyth*

*Debbie Bias*

*Lydia Smith*

*Erika Beumer*

*Helen Allen*

*Paula Williams*

Thank you to the editors that helped me when I was going to give up. **Christine Beech**, **Jo Wildsmith, Anne Anderson** and **Matthew Bird**.

**Michael Heppell** and his Write That Book Masterclasses have been so helpful and continue to be helpful. I never thought for a minute that I would have written five books. But the support and confidence the group offers is just fantastic. I have made friends for life too.

# About the Author

Fiona Myles Scottish through and through, living in Salford, I began writing as a child and it petered off after a while. I have always been good at writing things and went into administration as a career. Was always the one called upon to write letters for things or articles for magazines.

The desire to write my story was fired up during lockdown by a friend of mine. Ending up writing three books in less than eighteen months. Connecting with Michael Heppell and the Write That Book crew really got my writing into first gear. I have another three books in the pipeline.

I am married to Brian and have one daughter and one stepson. We love going on great outdoor adventures with our little dog Sparkles.

# OTHER BOOKS BY FIONA MYLES

Fiona Myles has also written four books around her adoption and Christian testimony.

## This is me - No Darkness Too Deep

Fiona writes very honestly and openly about her life before becoming a Christian and of her life as a Christian. She shares about how it is not all rosy in life just because you are a Christian.

## This is Me - I'm Adopted

Fiona again writes with an openness about her adoption and infertility issues. Going on to share about how God brought her a child at 50 years of age.

## Adoption Trauma

Discovering that Adoption Trauma was a thing. Fiona set about writing about her feelings as a child and young adult as an adoptee. The feelings of abandonment, not fitting in, looking different. Through stories and poetry this book lays out what adoption trauma can feel like with some great self-care routines within the pages too.

## Georgie Me & ADHD

A Mother's story about the difficulties parents of SEN children can face.

All available on **Amazon**